An Analysis of the Royal Preserves in Portugal

ISSUES OF PRIVILEGE, POWER, MANAGEMENT, AND CONFLICT

Cristina Joanaz de Melo

Translation into English by Sofia Barreto Leitão, Pedro Freire & by Wildtrack Publishing

ISBN 978-1-904098-54-6

Published by:
Wildtrack Publishing,
Venture House,
103 Arundel Street,
Sheffield S1 2NT
UK

Typeset and processed by Christine Handley

"The photographs of the tiles showing hunting scenes were shot in the lobby of the Municipal Library of Braga. The photographs belong to me. Wildtrack is allowed to publish them, anytime, anywhere." Cristina Joanaz de Melo.

Front cover photograph: © Cristina Joanaz de Melo.

© **Wildtrack Publishing and Author 2015.**

All rights reserved. No part of this publication may be reproduced or transmitted in any form or by any means, electronic or mechanical, including photocopying, recording, or any information storage or retrieval system, without permission in writing from the publisher.

Table of Contents

CONVENTIONS AND ABBREVIATIONS ... 1
Introductory note ... 3
INTRODUCTION ... 7
   Setting the scene ... 7
   Relevance and state of the art ... 14
1. EVOLUTION OF FOREST AND HUNTING LAW: GENERAL LAWS AND RESERVES ... 21
   1.1. In the Ancient Regime ... 21
      1.1.1. General system and reserve system ... 21
      1.1.2. Hunting and forest law ... 24
      1.1.3. Royal reserves ... 28
   1.2. The Liberal Revolution: disruption or continuity? ... 46
2. RESOURCE MANAGEMENT: AGRARIAN AND HUNTING EXPLOITATION 51
   2.1. Royal reserves: "wild" space and "tamed" space ... 51
   2.2. Contracts and licences ... 53
   2.3. Evolution of reserve management ... 55
      2.3.1. Farming and forest resources ... 55
      2.3.2. Game resources ... 71
3. PRIVILEGES AND CONFLICTS ... 77
   3.1. Aristocratic ethos and hunting ... 78
   3.2. Royal stays ... 84
   3.3. Social conflicts ... 92
      3.3.1. Hunting ... 93
      3.3.2. Undergrowth and timber ... 112
CONCLUSIONS ... 118
Surveyor-Generals of His Majesty's Woods and Forests ... 123
Brief chronology ... 123
GENERAL SOURCES ... 128
SPECIFIC BIBLIOGRAPHY ... 130
GENERAL BIBLIOGRAPHY ... 132

Acknowledgements

For timeless support, encouragement and trust beyond dimension: **To my family**

For then and now, in words that can not reach enough gratefulness,
to my MA Supervisor, friend and advisor: Luis Espinha da Silveira.

Specifically in this work, both for scientific encouragement, pushing forward in accuracy as for friendship:

Christine Handley
Ian Rotherham

Helder Carvalho
Hugo Silva
Luisa Luzio
Nuno Camarinhas
Nuno Monteiro

Marcus Hall who always pushed me forward to chase any subject I liked, especially when it brings me joy.

For their patience, work (translation / revision) and friendship to: Sofia Leitão Sondergaard (2000), Pedro Bento Freire (2013), Miriam Nogueira Santos (2013), Constança Bobone (2015).

To all the friends and colleagues that heard me talking and talking endlessly hours after hours, years after years about hunting and the joy it brings.

Lisbon, July 2015
Cristina

CONVENTIONS AND ABBREVIATIONS

Bibliographic quotes are presented in full only at the first reference.
The number of footnotes is continuous from the first to the fifth chapter.

References to the *Regimento da Montaria-Mor do Reino de 1605* (Regulations of the Surveyor-General's Department of 1605), published by Baeta Neves in the *Anais do Instituto Superior de Agronomia,* the *Regimento das Matas, Coutadas, Montarias e Defesas* (Regulations of Woods, Reserves, Parks, and Enclosed Grounds) of September 27th 1650, published in the set of legislation by José Justino de Andrade e Silva, and the *Regimento de 1800* (Regulations of 1800), published in the set of legislation by António Delgado da Silva, will be presented as follows after the first reference: Regulations of the Surveyor-General's Department of 1605, or Regulations of 1605; Regulations of Woods, Reserves, Parks, and Enclosed Grounds, or Regulations of 1650; and Regulations of 1800, or New Regulations on Reserves, respectively.

All legislation indicated that is not part of the Surveyor-General's Department is taken from Silva, António Delgado da – *Colecção de Legislação Portuguesa desde a Última Compilação das Ordenações*, 6 vols., Lisbon, 1825-1830.

One last note about the abbreviations used and how documents of the Surveyor-General's Department were quoted:

ANTT – Arquivo Nacional da Torre do Tombo (National Archive)
BNL – Biblioteca Nacional de Lisboa (National Library)
MMR – Montaria-Mor do Reino (Surveyor-General's Department) – Nucleus of the Surveyor-General's Department of the Arquivo Histórico do Ministério do Planeamento, Equipamento e Administração do Território, former Ministério das Obras Públicas (Historical Archive of the Planning, Equipment and Territorial Administration Office, former Public Works Office)

The Historical Archive of the present Planning, Equipment and Territorial Administration Office, former Public Works Office, maintains the previous abbreviation of the office (MOP) identification of its documents. To avoid terminology ambiguities, rather than using the abbreviation AHMPEAT – Arquivo Histório do Ministério do Planeamento, Equipamento e Administração do Território, which does not appear in any of the documents analysed at the time this investigation took place, as can be seen in one of the maps reproduced in this work, the decision was to use the abbreviation of the nucleus of documents of the Surveyor-General's Department, which belongs to the archive of the present office:

MMR-x-Book 1 or 2 – date, where: *MMR* stands for the nucleus of the Montaria-Mor do Reino (Surveyor-General's Department), x is the series number, Book 1 or 2 is self-explanatory, and date is the date of the document.

The series classed in boxes were organised in chronological order by year, semester, and day. The packets are ordered chronologically by 1st and 2nd semester, and the documents are ordered by day, month, and year. So, the reference to loose documents is indicated as follows: nucleus, series, year, and date of the document. For example, MMR-16-1779-01.06.1779.

Introductory note

In the 1990s, the Portuguese historiography on the period at the end of the eighteenth century and in the early 1800s saw significant progress in several areas related to the theme of this book.

In fact, throughout that decade important studies about the state, aristocracy and seigniorial regime have been published. Concerning the first topic, the research showed that the administrative apparatus in the service of the monarchy had a low number of officers and was unable to exercise effective control over the territory. The territorial division was marked by extreme discontinuity of administrative and judicial units, reflecting the plurality of the existing powers (the crown, the secular and ecclesiastical lords and municipalities). This did not easily assert dominion over space to the monarchy that it attempted to affirm, above all, from the second half of the eighteenth century onwards. Indeed, on the outskirts, the power was concentrated in the hands of local elites that ruled over municipalities. In the second half of the 1700s, the Crown was trying to master that same power that it had favoured for a long time.

At the top of Portuguese society was the King and his court, made up of about sixty aristocratic houses. This high nobility, largely created by the dynasty of Braganza, which had ascended the throne in 1640, was settled in Lisbon. The aristocracy was living mainly off income from property donated by the Kings in exchange for services rendered to the Crown, thus generating mutual ties and complicity of dependence. This nobility was deeply rentier in its economic relationships and had very weak bonds with their estates and the people living there.

In part of those lands of the royal family, the aristocracy, the military orders and religious houses, the seigniorial regime was very harsh. Yet, this regime was far from covering most of the territory of Portugal on the European continent. Actually, it was extremely strong only for the peasants living within the country's central coastal areas, between Lisbon, Santarem, Coimbra and Aveiro, reaching an area that in certain places widened slightly further inland.

The knowledge of these fundamental features of Portuguese society at the end of the Ancient Regime, here generically referred, was essential to identify some of the specific characteristics of the Portuguese Liberal Revolution. In fact, this was marked, not by a struggle between the central government and the regional powers which did not exist, but rather the conflict between the centre and the local municipal / county powers. The extreme social exclusiveness and deep dependence of the aristocracy in relation to the Crown facilitated the fight against the liberal nobility, in respect to which the Portuguese revolution was very radical. Finally, the revolution extinguished the manorial regime on behalf of private property and of a capitalist economy, but this was not accompanied by a broad anti-manorial peasant movement.

It is this intellectual context that frames the Master's thesis from Cristina Joanaz de Melo as the origin of the book now being published. Its interest lies in the chosen subject, the royal game reserves of forest and hunting, an issue which at the time (1990s), was virtually unstudied. The research was then focused on the end of the period of the Ancient Regime and the first attempt to implement a liberal regime in Portugal, trying to understand the continuities and ruptures operated by change of political regime.

The issue is addressed in various perspectives: the duty applicable to game reserves, the management of funds of the same, the use of game reserves as an area of court life and the monarchy government as a source stated at the time, and finally, the land dispute, plants and animals of these territories, which is expressed through common crime.

The contribution of this volume was to highlight the importance of the actual game reserves, because of their significant land area and the heavy restrictions that this system imposed on all those who lived in the preserves. This sheds light on a lesser-known aspect of the manorial system. The relevance of these spaces reserved for the production of wood for shipbuilding and farmed game, impelled the Crown to create their own service, the Montaria-Mor do Reino (the General Administration for the Royal Preserves of the Kingdom), provided with staff dedicated to the management of resources, policing body and judges with jurisdiction over crimes committed inside the royal parks, wetlands and woodlands, allowing the Kings to assert their authority over a vast area of the territory, with the limits that the study analyses. This work also revealed the importance of game reserves in the annual cycle of court visits and social distinction associated with various hunting practices. Finally, confirming the value of the resources in question and the weight of the limitations to the cultivation of land, grazing, collecting wood and hunting, even in defence of the land cultivated on the edge of game reserves, this study shows us the variety of crimes and trespasses practiced every day, ranging from the release of forest fires, the illegal sale of timber and poaching. These activities involve an extensive list of agents that included the officers of the General Administration of the Royal Preserves, peasants, clergy and members of local elites who live in the villages of game reserves. It is this whole universe of people, groups, institutions, as the relationships established between them lay around the forest and hunting resources in the space of real preserves that this book carefully documents and reveals.

It was certainly no accident that the extinction of the royal hunting preserves was one of the first steps taken in 1821 by the newly open Liberal parliament with regard to the manor system. It is also no coincidence that a part of the area of the royal preserves on the left bank of the Tagus River near Lisbon, is today one of the most important reserves of Europe's birds. Interestingly, a sign of the times in which they lived, another of these game reserves gave rise in 1836, to one of the (nowadays) oldest agricultural companies in the country.

The study Cristina Joanaz de Melo completed in 1998 was motivated by the interest of the author for the management of natural resources. This interest had a second expression in her doctoral thesis defended in 2010 at the European University Institute in Florence. This was entitled "Against Floods and Storms: Spatial Awareness, Parliamentary Debate and Water Policies and Forests in Portugal (1852-1886) "and is still alive in their most recent work, with which it has given an important contribution to the development of the History of Environment in Portugal.

Louis Espinha da Silveira,
Department of History,
Faculty of Social and Human Sciences,
Universidade Nova de Lisboa,
Lisbon, July 2015.

"Whoever looks through this text will feel he jumped outside dates and History, transported into a universe that knows the alternation of day and night, as well as the passing of seasons, but knows nothing of the clock of centuries (...). Behold a world one finds once again with a beat of one's heart, every time, having left at dawn, one sees a young goat going around at the edge of the woods or young foxes playing on the grass. Behold the marks of the horseshoe or the claw on the sand, the water drunk by sunset, the eyes shining under the leaves, the rut entwining wild lovers in the forest; behold the different breeds of dogs; behold the people of horses, heroic subjects faithful to humans. Behold the innocent lion that quietly tears to pieces its prey; behold the deer standing, its neck stretched to protect its herd, a black shadow against the paleness of daybreak..."

That Mighty Sculptor, Time, Marguerite Yourcenar

INTRODUCTION

Setting the scene

In 1998, with an initial volume published in Portugal 2000, I presented the conclusions of my MA dissertation from which this book derives. Following that outcome, I studied the functioning and symbolic meanings of the royal preserves, parks, and forests in a transitional period of Portuguese political regimes: at the end of the Ancient Regime and on the aftermath of the first liberal revolution in Portugal (1821), from 1777 to 1824.

The choice of the chronological barriers set was essentially due to the aim defined at the beginning of the research: understanding how life developed in royal reserves before and after the Liberal Revolution. As the majority of works on hunting in Modern Ages produced before 1998 were on hunting and royal preserves in England, Spain or France, the analysis was planned, accordingly to the *classical* approach of looking at this theme through the lens of aristocratic social attributes of disposing preserves. If the classic *Whigs and Hunters* from E. P. Thompson proclaimed the prerogatives of aristocracy for the British aristocracy mastering of property rights, *status* and *ethos*, other contributions of the preserves regime, in the mastering of social order and in the attempt to balance or master powers, can be added, for other regions in Europe. In this case, the focus is on Portugal.

The process of the judicial, administrative and police reforms started in Portuguese royal parks, woodlands, woods, under the governance and reign of the Queen D. Maria I (1777-1792). Her son D. João VI (regent in 1792) did show a different "use" of the royal preserves. In the Portuguese monarchy in this period, the reform of the Royal Preserves apparatus and resources management, took place in a broader movement for the empowerment of the Crown above aristocracy through the dilution of seigniorial powers.

In Portuguese studies, it has been stated that a major cornerstone for the imbalance of power in favour of the crown, in 1790, was the decree that abolished the ecclesiastical and seigniorial judicial competences[1]. This Act subjucated all judicial entities to the royal ones. If this meant there was a deep injury in seigniorial autonomy towards the monarch, somehow in the Portuguese royal preserves this process had already began in 1777, or even before in the course of the Modern Ages.

During this era, in Portugal, the royal preserves and the royal parks would evolve into a wide variety of meanings and uses: administrative, judicial, and even political. I would dare to propose that local conflicts, and those in the royal parks and woodlands with other seigniorial justices and jurisdictions, would become not only wanted, but also necessary and useful. These placed the King above all other Modern social bodies. In the way it happened in Portugal, something similar could have evolved in French, Spanish and Italian states, also following absolutist regimes, to master the local balance of powers.

Considering a society of corporations to whom different niches of power had been granted there was a permanent need to reduce the power of anyone blocking the monarch's authority. Thus, one of the peculiarities about the Portuguese Kings' symbolic authority beyond the forest acts and hunting affairs was the exclusive right of the monarch to create and take back preserves. Legally, the capacity to implement preserves and to master regulations for them, provided the King with a tool, at the level of exercising justice, to place himself above aristocracy and clerical institutions[2] as to distribute grace and protection.

Already in the 16th century, D. João III found a way, through hunting procedures, of slightly breaking the judicial untouched authority within the seigniorial estates. In 1549, the King created the obligation of hunting predators twice a year in all counties of the realm, in his estates as in other seigniorial and ecclesiastical ones. In the end, it would be more or less respected.

Yet in 1575, the cork oak trees regimen imposed across fairly half of the area of the Tagus River water basin (in Portugal) in the king's estates as over seigniorial ones was somehow a strong statement of power of the monarch over the aristocracy and church land rights. In the Modern Ages this was not a minor issue. By this law, none could fell cork oak trees without the royal forests bureaux license. Those trees had been reserved strictly for the royal service of the navy, independent from the social origin and prerogatives of their landowners. The overseas empire then became, unavoidably linked to woodland management and raw materials for shipbuilding and some stocks distributed across aristocratic estates, were included in the timber monopoly of the crown. An equivalent measure took place in France almost one century later. The (well-known) Colbert Act of 1669[3], with similar implications was passed in the reign of Louis XIV.

It is noteworthy that almost one century earlier the Portuguese crown had already demonstrated the capacity to take back property land rights from the aristocracy, including rights of forest management. It is also true that one might assume a link to the taking of timber rights for shipbuilding and a conflict with use for aristocratic / church estates with development of the overseas Empire; though it could have compensations. Maybe the landowners, from the church and the aristocracy, affected by the reservation of cork trees could be rewarded with a high position in the Empire. Yet it was not the case for all, and certainly not for the biggest aristocratic house of Portuguese nobility, the Duke of Cadaval. This estate, from 1808-1820, was still obeying the rule that prevented the cutting of trees considered useful for royal service (see later).

Archive research on the timber issue suggests controls across the royal estates and beyond in the areas preserved for the royal navy throughout the Modern Age. Nonetheless, further research is required to confirm or deny such assertions. What is beyond doubt is that greater or weaker presence of the royal family, and consequently the court, in the preservation of large game and birds directly influenced density and quality of poaching during the dynasties of Avis (1385 - 1580), Hapsburg (1580 - 1640) and Bragança (1640 - 1910).

In the 18th century, during the fifty years of the D. João V reign (1695 – 1750), preserves for large game (wild boar and deer) as far as the margins of the Tagus River, were cherished and controlled as never before. This period of strong royal presence of the Court in Salvaterra de Magos was followed by a time of less frequent visits by the royal family and aristocracy during the reign of D. José I (1750 - 1777). Gradually, a reduced presence of the royal influence and power across those lands led to increased poaching in the majority of the parks and woodlands.

When the Queen D. Maria started her reign, the symbolic estates of royal privilege were in chaos, with respect to the seigniorial rules and limits. Trespasses had almost become the rule with limited consequences for the corrupt judges of the royal preserves of game or timber, or for the administrative staff, keepers, and prison guards. The beginning of reform from 1777 - 1882, recognised the attempt to re-assert the Queen's undoubted desire to hold authority over her hunting and woodlands estates. This was achieved in complex ways, as will be further explored. This included the reviewing processes for replacing the officers under the control of the queen, for nominating new staff, and for the administration of appointments of magistrates and keepers. There was also the imprisonment of corrupt officers, the latter having become the biggest poachers of all.

The picture looks rather different from the Modern Age attempts of monarchs to use forest and hunting affairs in the royal preserves and estates, covering approximately 22% of Portugal. The geographical area under the direct administration of the king in the Portuguese territory, suggested that the monarchs were above the other social bodies of the Ancient Regime. Furthermore, the royal preserves' organisation had its own courts dealing with all legal conflicts involving forest and hunting issues. In the data scrutinized in the archive in the *book of the royal preserves correspondence* from 1521 to 1833 and in the documentation analysed from 1777 to 1824, there was no single process involving the Holy Inquisition. That would be an interesting topic to develop intensively for there were animals forbidden by the church as food, like crabs and lobsters, since they were not mentioned in the Book of Genesis and had the appearance of demons[4] as other mammals with horns allowed as food as large game.

In a Catholic Monarchy, and especially under D. Maria I, government was strictly accordingly to the precepts of Rome, with no evidence of interference by the Highest Court in crimes and trials relating to the preserved forest, ponds, fisheries. Apparently, in both social and religious affairs, symbolic as well as effective power was held exclusively by the Queen. Indeed, sometime before, in the 16th century and until 1750, judicial disputes on forest and poaching trespasses in the royal preserves and on their borders with other estates were between members of gentry, clergymen, and officers from municipalities or local military bodies. These were decided personally by the royal appointees. In other words, in the realm of D. Maria I, the administrative and juridical system to manage royal woodlands and parks, went far beyond the seigniorial order of the time.

From 1777, in the Queen's lands reserved for hunting and timber, there was a widening of judicial control over other bodies of justice. Permission was given for the Queen's Keepers to shoot all poachers regardless of their social strata. This included aristocrats and ecclesiastical persons with a strengthening of trials on poaching with new judges appointed directly from the supreme court of the Crown. This confirmed the authority to decide upon such affairs above religious, gentry, municipal, and of craft corporations and contributed to improved order. Unlike any other model for the administration of preserves in Europe, D. Maria I had an institution at her disposal with officials that could extend across the necessary territory. This was in part through the established municipal hunting of predators that was carried out, irregularly, over time. The degree of conflict arising between the officers from of the royal preserves when such tasks were attempted, within or beyond the preserves, was a measure of the acceptance or disrespect of royal officers across the monarch's estates. This was also the case on aristocratic and ecclesiastical seigniorial lands. This structure already existed and so, in the 1780s, the excuse to proceed with killing of wolves and foxes made it feasible to enlist the population in the undertaking. This involved the making of lists of people, fit and unfit, for physical work and for poaching.

Despite these efforts, the killing of wolves and foxes would barely surpass earlier attempts. Very often, as outsiders, the Judges of the preserves were received with open aggression from local people . Nonetheless, reporting the results of these forays was compulsory. Compiled at the central services of the royal preserves organisation, the information about such failures or successes provides feedback on geographical and social aspects of conflicts. Aside from the use of the administration and officials of the royal preserves to subjugate local communities and weaken seigniorial powers, the reigns of D. Maria I and D. João VI were affected by other factors. Significant external events influenced the administration of royal reserves.

In relation to the Portuguese Empire, in 1777, D. Maria began her reign facing wars in the colonies, and particularly in the frontiers of Brazil. This was an important territory, which had been a good supplier of timber for the royal fleet. However, that huge region was viewed with envy by other European powers. Amongst other serious losses that threatened, like the gold region and the frontiers in the south, the timber supply was at risk if Brazil was lost. Therefore, the supply of timber became imperative, at any cost in the metropolis, to maintain communication links with the empire, and assure means of defence and combat at sea. Furthermore, in the aftermath of the French Revolution (1789), the destruction of Versailles with its immense hunting and woodland preserves had been a very powerful blow against the monarchies of Europe more generally. As a response, in the other autocratic monarchies, aristocracy and seigniorial rights were to be reinforced, and the symbolic estates of privilege, game parks, and other hunting lands, were to be kept. This was presumably to represent a sign of untouched royal authority.

When D. João VI, son of D. Maria I, came to power in 1792, hunting preserves would be managed according to this same principle. Even though the King preferred the wetlands for bird and duck shooting, the parks and woods for game breeding were to be administered under very strict rules. On the other hand, even when the war in Brazil was controlled, threats against the royal navy prevailed in the Atlantic and still the timber preserves needed to be carefully managed.

Yet, in 1807, ejected by the armies of Napoleon, the royal family and the court moved to Brazil. French attempts to occupy Portugal occurred from 1808 to 1812. Helped by the English, Napoleon's army was contained in 1812 and the British administration left Portugal in 1820. Under the short French administration, as afterwards during the British one, the royal preserves were maintained as before for recreation and shipbuilding. Throughout the first two decades of the 19th century, the preserves remained essential as they were. There was continuing need for timber and charcoal supplies for war and defence, for housing consumption, and for smelting lead. These remained intense or probably increased. With the end of Napoleonic wars, and the departure of the British administration (1820), the Liberal Order was to change core prerogatives of social control by granting individual property rights and abolishing privileges. This might also mean the end of central control over forest resource monopolies.

In 1821, under the Liberal consulate, the game preserves were abolished before even the seigniorial rights. However, with the return of the Absolutism (1823), seigniorial rights were recovered (1824); and with these, the royal privileges on the preserves. The management and monopoly over raw materials, essential for various activities beyond local controls, were also restored in favour of the crown.

Yet, in the absence of the crown, the royal forests were kept for timber under the administrative system of public service. This was in line with what had happened in France (1789), where the royal forests were transferred to National ownership trusted to the State management. In fact, with the return of the absolutist political regime in 1823, and in the course of the following year of 1824, the General Administration for the Royal Forests was created for the management of the national forests. Such organisation endured until 1881. It survived the abolishment of the Ancient Regime (1828-32), civil wars, liberal civil wars for the implementation of a bi-cameral elective Regime, the inclusion of the King as part of the ruling system (1834 - 1851), and afterwards under the consolidated Constitutional monarchy until 1881.

From 1777 on, and until 1821, when the Constitutional Assembly abolished seigniorial rights in Portugal, the administration of the royal preserves produced continuous, abundant and well-organised information on royal reserves. However, it is only in 1824, with the restoration of the Ancient Regime's legislation that the first Portuguese liberal period ended. The reaction of the Liberal legislator in abolishing the reserves for hunting and preserving the ones for timber as "National Forests", allows us to understand the real strategic importance of forest resources in the population's economy and their symbolic meaning in the global re-establishment of seigniorial rights.

This book is structured to address how, by the end of the Ancient Regime, the Preserves bureau had acquired the authority to help the process of strengthening the Crown's undisputed influence across the entire realm. This control was over all social strata including high nobility, estates, clergy, and municipalities. Considering the issues noted earlier, this work seeks to develop aspects regarding the economic dimension of the royal reserves, namely its management, as well as the legal and illegal exploitation of its goods. An attempt is also made to understand the reasons for social conflict and to study the different kinds of confrontations arising from the dispute of resources. This is bound by the idea of competition among social bodies for the control of local power. In this context, the Surveyor-General's Department is also analysed, in terms of what it represented as an institution and as a power rooted in the territory - in permanent conflict with all social agents, from the Crown's appointees to the country's jurisdiction - as well as concerning the power relationships established between its officers, court aristocracy, provincial nobility, municipalities, and peasants.

Then, in Chapters 1, 2 and 3, the functioning of the numerous entities living inside the preserves, and the broader meaning of what the extension of those areas represented in terms of the capacity of the King to give or take back seigniorial regimes to aristocrats are analysed.

The conclusions highlight the relevance of the role of royal preserves for strengthening the rising authority of the crown over other social bodies. The work considers how this served the purposes of administrative royal centralization during the late Ancient Regime in Portugal. Finally, the study addresses how the structure of a centralized body created in the 16th century endured as a model for the building up of the centralized administrative Liberal Sate.

Relevance and state of the art

Throughout the Middle Ages, in the British Isles, and in French, Spanish and Portuguese territories, as a space of privilege, the royal parks had a very distinguished symbolic meaning. Indeed, almost all analyses explore the forest and hunting issues through the lens of privilege or of ecological resilience.

One topic left aside in the historical debate on centralization is the importance of the institutions for the management of parks and forests in this process. One can also observe that studies in political, social, economic, or agrarian history for Modern Ages Portugal ignore the role of forest laws and the organisation of the preserves at the level of the centralized as well as the local and seigniorial administration. In a less challenging way, one might consider that hunting, forest acts and royal reserves' administration only played a modest contribution to counter-balance powers at the local level as well as at court[5].

It is necessary to verify the complexity of social and institutional relationships that the reserve regime involved, as well as the geographical, political, and administrative range of the royal preserves in the Portuguese territory throughout the Modern Ages. The study then considers the importance of that structure in the build-up of royal institutions beyond their originally allocated powers.

Although presenting different approaches on these topics, work on Spanish, French, and English cases has focused on social, economic, and ecological values of forest laws and the importance of parks and woodlands. This is more-so than for the Portuguese situation. Research has highlighted the mosaic of medieval patterns of organisation as modern social and economic systems with symbolic importance[6].

Until the end of the 20th century, among the French, British, or Spanish studies, produced regarding hunting and forests for deer breeding throughout the Middle and Modern

Ages, many approached the theme from the perspective of lending social status. Under this approach, game and forest laws were established to benefit seigniorial and lordship privileges[7].

However, less has been written about the importance of these same subjects in what concerns the process of strengthening the power of the Crown against aristocracy, or in subsuming medieval forms of local powers.

Such developments sometimes occurred in a later period than in Portugal, for example, in the 17th century for the French case. The famous Colbert Law of 1669 took back the rights not only of the French aristocracy in forestry but of all the communities living inside the borders of the forest 'fit for shipbuilding'[8]. In Portugal, this process began with the Cork Oak Forest Act of 1575, determining cork as monopoly of the Crown in the Tagus watershed.

In the studies noted in the bibliography, even the acts that preserved timber for the royal navy, the Colbert Act of 1669 mentioned before, have been analysed as an act of acquired absolute power over, in this case, the French nobility. Nevertheless, what was the relevance and the internal impact of such control? Would it follow the same path as the pioneer of these kind of acts, promulgated in 1575 in Portugal where such rules had already been performed over the previous two centuries? Indeed, there is no such information on hunting and forest history for the Middle, Modern, or Contemporary eras.

In the last decade, there have been numerous contributions on the history of forest and hunting in Britain from ecology, economy, forestry, archaeology, arc-science, environmental, and social disciplines[9]. Adding an ecological approach to this vision, other works have established how parks for venison, and forest law privileges, became important in nature conservation, as well as for farming. Moreover, the multi-functional special bodies created to manage venison and timber reserves, with keepers, judges and administrative staff, in France, Spain, Britain, or Portugal contributed to social and environmental achievements. These outputs included aristocratic preservation of status through forest privileges, conservation of pristine landscapes, and efficient management in woodlands and on farmland.

Independent from these contributions, none seems to have addressed the role of royal forest organisation in contributing to the weakening of the powers of social bodies, local communities, and the Church.

The most recent history of hunting in France, edited by Andrée Corvol (2010), or the 1st Congress on Hunting, held in Paris in 2003, did not address any of these issues. However, they did present new approaches anchored in symbolic meanings and not in the practical uses of forest institutions as agents for strengthening the royal power in peripheral areas. In this ground-breaking congress hunting practices were mostly approached as translating behaviours of social classes, groups, or bodies. Even iconographic representation stated an existing reality, with for example, images of hunting practices designed as eternal law that endured through the pictures. In my view, as written laws, the painted images of hunting practices were visual codes showing everyone how social order should always be.

Another approach was through the creation of royal preserves as a sign of undisputed authority. This interpretation might apply in Spain, when in 1624, Filipe IV created new hunting parks, or in France when in 1669, Louis XIV with Colbert took back rights on forests from the aristocracy. Both situations transferred rights and confirmed the effective power of the kings over the aristocracy. In Portugal, this same process happened, but it occurred much earlier. This was not only from *above* but also because the distribution of land, rents, both seigniorial and church, came under the administration of the crown by the 15th century. This occurred legally and without any break from the church in Rome. The political and religious processes through which the Crown gained the mastership of military orders was not through conflict with the aristocracy.

The mastership of the military orders should belong to a prince of royal blood. In the late 15th century, the future Dom Manuel I, the 6th in the line of succession unexpectedly became king. The other candidates for the throne died under plots allegedly against the crown and also of natural causes. Dom Manuel ascended to the throne. From that moment on, the crown reunited the administration of lands belonging to the military orders and the royal family estates. The royal family became the owner of the largest area of land administration together with the monopoly of the overseas Empire. No other aristocratic house could ever again compete with the royal family. Controlling a new significant amount of properties, throughout the 16th century, the royal family expanded preserved areas for deer and wild boar hunting, on the right and left banks of the River Tagus. It was in this process of expansion of land and preserves that the structure needed to manage forests was created and was improved according to new needs. And, all this process also requires further study for the Modern Ages in Portugal.

There is little published literature on royal reserves, or even on the history of hunting and forest in Portugal. Worthy of reference, by chronological order are the following: 1) Carlos Riley's study, *Sobre a Caça Medieval*[10], which considers hunting in Portugal but is not a detailed study of a specific territory; 2) Maria Leonor Costa's study, *Naus e Galeões na Ribeira de Lisboa*[11], where the author analyses the sources of the timber used in boat construction; 3) *História Florestal, Aquícola e Cinegética* and 4) the article "Dos Monteiros Mores aos Engenheiros Silvicultores" that registers the works of Carlos Manuel Baeta Neves, pioneer in the history of hunting and forest in Portugal[12]; 5) The book on the correspondence carried out between D. Filipe I of Spain and his daughter, married to the Portuguese king, published by Fernando Bouza and edited by this author, Nuno Senos, Antonio Hespanha and Pedro Cardim, describes the hunting trips extensively. Yet the editors focus on other issues different from the importance of the administrative structure for hunting affairs[13] and 6) the two articles by Nicole Devy-Varetta where an attempt is made to create a "historical geography of the Portuguese forest"[14]. The latter refers to the late Middle Ages and the Renaissance and draw maps of a part of the royal reserves. This latter author also presents a brief chronology of the constitution of reserves and develops the history of the use of wood in royal reserves, in her work *A Floresta no Espaço e no Tempo em Portugal – A Arborização da Serra da Cabreira (1919 - 1975)*[15]. António Manuel Hespanha, in his study *As Vésperas do Leviathan*[16], only briefly considers some of the legislation on the constitution of reserves and their management in the Ancient Regime. More recently, in 2009, Felix Labrador Arroyo, in his book on the Royal House in Portugal 1580-1621 (*La Casa Real en Portugal 1580-1621*) touches on the issue of the hunting trips of the royal family, the king's council and the court, in a wider context of the Royal House networking, as part of something bigger[17].

In Spain, these subjects have been considered in more detail than in Portugal. Several authors, like Count Yebes and Ortega y Gasset, have treated the subject with a philosophical approach, whereas authors like Lopez Ontiveros[18] and Maria José Rúbio Aragonés[19] have presented a historical perspective.

Regarding forest history, the Spanish school has mainly investigated the public estates (*montes*) that became State property, after the process of selling the estate in 1869. Research prior to this date is scarce. In France, as in Spain, works on hunting and the history of hunting, as well as on forest history, are more extensively analysed for the Ancient Regime and Liberalism periods than in Portugal, or Britain. For this subject, reference to Philippe Salvadori's doctoral thesis, published in 1996 is essential. This work is a history of hunting during the Ancient Regime in France, with special focus on the French royal reserves, approaching the study in the longterm under the perspective of hunting as seigniorial privilege[20].

In the British case, a lot more has been offered to the academic and general public, for the Middle, Modern, and Contemporary Ages, since the seminal work of E. P. Thompson, *Whigs and Hunters*. Despite lagging behind British academic output on hunting affairs, French and Spanish research has produced few but very interesting works on hunting studies and the impact of preserves officers in the territories. However, the importance of this activity for the aristocracy of the Modern Ages was such a passionate subject that Salvadori described the 16th and 17th centuries as the "Golden Centuries of French Hunting"[21]. Maria José Rúbio Aragonés even claims that Madrid became the capital city of Spain because it was the place where the King stayed most often, considering it the best game reserves regularly visited by the Habsburgs[22].

Embedded in political moves to push aside or take over recognized religious authority to control society, art became the most efficient tool to express the escalating independence of aristocratic classes all over Europe. These were direct competitors to the religious orders sponsoring masterpieces of architecture or paintings endorsing laic contexts, that is to say, paying for monumental civil architecture and paintings[23].

Indeed, it was during the 16th and 17th centuries that the game reserves of the French and Spanish courts expanded and the construction of great castles and palaces was encouraged. This was the case in both in catholic and protestant countries. Good examples of this monumental representation of the self and the power attached to it would be the Castle of Chambord in France; designed by Leonardo Da Vinci for Francis I. Other examples would be the Escorial and the Prado, built for the Kings of Spain. In Austria, Emperor Frederic the Wise chose Lucas Cranach to portray the aristocracy in hunting scenes. In Spain, Velasquez represented the Spanish Habsburg dynasty wearing hunting attire.

Whether in pictures or in architectural monuments from the "Golden Centuries of Hunting"[24] the hunt is portrayed as an important daily activity. This kept its vitality amongst the imperial houses of Europe until the end of the Ancient Regime.

In the Portuguese case, the passion for hunting activities is visible throughout the entire Ancient Regime. The majority of the royal reserves date from the late 16th century and were created by King D. Sebastião I in the last quarter ov 1500s[25]. They were confirmed with almost all their extensions by the Habsburg dynasty (under the united crown of Portugal and Spain 1580-1640) in the Regulations of the Surveyor-General's Department of 1605. This was alongside the safeguarding of an extensive overseas empire within the Portuguese and Spanish territories. The fleet was to be increased, and therefore a huge amount of timber would be required to supply the royal navy. Royal reserves and activities for the maintenance of the forest increased, as a characteristic of the royal statute, driven by economic and logistic imperative.

As with other European monarchies, like the French and Spanish, in the beginning of the 17th century Felipe II of Portugal created an organisation specialised in the defence of the Crown's forest and hunting property. This was the Surveyor-General's Department of His Majesty's Woods and Forests and was maintained by the Portuguese Bragança dynasty until the end of the Ancient Regime[26].Fortunately this institution produced a great amount of data preserved to the present. The documentation used to produce this work came fundamentally from the Surveyor-General's Department. Therefore, in most cases the perspective provided is that of the Crown's institution created to protect the Crown's interests. Only through some petitions and other processes was it possible to have access to different perspectives[27]. As a reference, this documentation consists mainly of official correspondence sent to and from the Surveyor-General's Department. It reports on the territory's administration and control, peasants' and officers' petitions, and judicial cases. Apart from this archive, other sources were used including some notes of the Surveyor-General's Department kept in the National Archive of the Torre do Tombo and in the Municipal Archive of Benavente.

Legislation from the Middle Ages was analysed by means of hunting treatises originally from this period, but followed through the entire Modern period. These included treatises on conduct, on agriculture, and on the forest. Finally, to complement the archive data, economic and political memoirs were consulted.

1. EVOLUTION OF FOREST AND HUNTING LAW: GENERAL LAWS AND RESERVES

1.1. In the Ancient Regime

If royal and seigniorial reserves allowed the safeguarding of a vast area of forest property of which we are all heirs today, in the Ancient Regime the reserve represented the formula of seigniorial domain imposing a greater number of conditions to the peasants' survival. As it maintains the charges on the agrarian production, and simultaneously forbids communities inside the reserves to use the forest's resources that complement farming and cattle rearing, it may strongly aggravate the conditions affecting survival in the rural environment.

1.1.1. General system and reserve system

Though this work is focused on the study of royal reserves at the end of the Ancient Regime, one has to go back to the medieval period in the analysis of forest and hunting law, since both regulation systems, the "general system" and the "reserve system", were created then.

The concept of the "general system" designated the laws which were codified in the Royal Ordinances and addressed forest and hunting laws applied to the whole country as opposed to being an autonomous code. The concept "preserve system" or "reserve system" designated a special regulation system, distinct from general laws, exclusively applied to reserves. Each reserve had its own private regulation system, which defined the natural resources subject to privilege and the ways in which they should be used. The two systems were applied to distinct social agents, and the hunting and forest law constituted a reflection of the socio-economic differentiation. Therefore, the application of a "differential" law resulted from distinct economic, social, and political factors.

Throughout the Middle and Modern Ages, the forest was a vital space for the practice of the arts of cavalry, which noted hunting as a preparation for war[28]. Fulfilling two different purposes, one economic and the other as affirmation of prestige, the use of barren ground resources was codified. On the one hand, the population in general was allowed to use those resources, but with rules to rationalise exploitation and avoid total destruction. On the other hand, differential hunting practices were established in order to sanction and reinforce the distinct social categories. Thus, the Portuguese medieval society created a double system of appropriation of "wild" resources such as hunting, water, or forest. This double system was in force simultaneously and lasted until the end of the Ancient Regime.

It is important to note the King's role in granting reserves. Royal Ordinances contained a disposition that gave the monarch the exclusive right to create a reserve; a right maintained, unaltered from D. João I's reign, until the Constitutional Assembly[29]. In the regulations made for the practice of hunting, the legislation for the population in general adopts the Roman Law which implies the application of the *res nulius* principle[30]. Applied to hunting this principle determines that the owner of a land parcel has no right of ownership over wild animals. These go around freely and as with water and the air are nobody's property[31]. The right of ownership over game is acquired at the exact moment when the hunter chases, wounds, or kills. In this way, Roman Law separated the right of ownership over game from the right of ownership over real estate.

However, as society evolved, there was a reformulation of the right of ownership over game, accomplished by the creation of the reserve system. This limited the number of animals that could be hunted to the space where they live, and limited their ownership to the owner of the land, excluding tenants and renters from this right[32]. By granting the right to hunt exclusively to the landowner, the reserve system followed the application of German hunting law.

As such, in Portugal, both systems, the Roman and the German, were enforced during the Ancient Regime, applied respectively to distinct social agents. Roman Law was the support of the legislation for the population in general. German Law, on the other hand, applied to the special situation of the reserve system, granting privileges to the top of the social hierarchy.

Along the whole Ancient Regime the application of the German Law to hunting, resulted in the free use and appropriation of barren ground resources exclusively by the owner[33]. This created numerous situations of tension between rural populations, the Crown's appointees, and the King.

In terms of the forest law, its conception originates from a slightly different perspective than that of hunting law. This is given the fact that the forest is immovable and in relation to the total physical elements that compose this natural space. The *res nulius* formula has no application to the Portuguese forest. Trees, thickets and the soil belong to someone: the Crown, a person receiving the gift of the rights, or a municipality. Wild animals moving freely only become someone's property at the moment when they are captured or wounded. However, unlike these, the forest is a fixed structure that can be owned for a long period.

Limitation to the use of the forest's multiple resources reduced rural populations living in and around reserves to very precarious living conditions. In wood reserves they were forbidden to use wood, collect twigs, cut down trees and bushes to burn, and had restrictions on access to pastures and moors to rear cattle. This system intended to guarantee the reserve's owner the use of goods for his own profit and to raise his revenue from the trade he could make through the sale of twigs and wood and from giving grants to collect wood from the ground, as well as the use of all other resources[34].

In game reserves, however, alongside these same conditions, communities had other restrictions. They were forbidden to hunt for their own profit and to destroy forest resources that constituted the natural habitats of game species. Peasants living in reserves had to pay for rights for their produce as defined by their landlords. Furthermore, they were forbidden to kill game species that might destroy their crops and thus eliminate the products subject to those rights[35].

In a more pragmatic than philanthropic gesture, D. José, "taken of Royal Pity" and "love" for his subjects, in 1754, issued for the communities of the royal reserve of Pera e Comporta, licences to cut the timber needed for their farming and to repair their barns. He felt sympathetic to the sufferings that prevented peasants from "peacefully cultivating and inhabiting the land", as well as the damage resulting to "my royal incomes, since once the harvest-fields are destroyed no more rights and dues paid by them exist, according to their leases"[36]. In 1778, D. Maria I renewed this disposition.

In that same reserve, by the end of the 18th century, an organised action against the existence of reserves took place. In 1778, in Pera e Comporta[37], poachers secretly promoted riots against hunting prohibitions, encouraging peasants to sign documents to demand the abolition of reserves by Queen D. Maria I. Rumours were spread in the reserve of Pinheiro affirming that the reserves had been abolished. The rage and indignation of the Surveyor-General, D. Fernando José de Melo, reached its climax and he ordered an investigation into the "strange movements" of "collecting signatures for the extinction of reserves". He ordered the gamekeeper of the reserve of Pinheiro to proceed "in this case to a serious and exact investigation and the arrest, under his royal order, of the aggressor of such an attack"[38].

As these examples indicate, the reserve system triggered violent conflicts between the guardians of (especially game reserves) and populations living inside reserves. In 1821, after the abolition of game reserves by the Constitutional Assembly, the inhabitants of Cantanhede rebelled against the abuse of the reserve rights practised by the Marquis of Marialva on his properties. The same happened with the inhabitants of Palmela and Montemor-o-Novo who claimed against the application of reserve rights[39].

If on the one hand, the reserve system protected and safeguarded natural resources (hunting, forest, or water resources), being more effective than general laws, on the other hand, it generated enormous social tensions. This followed the application of privilege to maintain the use of resources exclusively to the owner and not with the purpose of protecting and managing wild resources for the use of the community.

1.1.2. Hunting and forest law

Having defined the general situation and the reserve systems, it is now time to explore the content of the hunting and forest laws in force between 1777 and 1824. These were expressed in the Royal Ordinances and further legislation not included in the ordinances.

By the end of the Ancient Regime, forest and hunting law were essentially identical to those proclaimed in the 16th century, during the reigns of D. João III and D. Sebastião, and later integrated in the Ordinances of D. Filipe II[40]. They regulated the rules of forestation, planting and treatment of trees, and hunting seasons, closed seasons, hunting techniques, instruments and guns that could be used by the population in general. They established the penalties to apply in cases of crimes committed against the forest and game.

The Ordinances of D. Filipe II imposed on local authorities the duty to promote tree planting to produce timber and fruit. Municipal councillors had the obligation to promote the plantation of pinewoods on estates and wastelands and "on the places that are not pinewoods they will have chestnuts, oaks and other trees planted"[41]. The royal magistrates' role was to have fruit trees[42] planted and grafted. Cutting fruit trees was an act punishable with whipping, and two years exile[43]. Together with local authorities, the Ordinances imposed for example, on landlords on the margins of the Tagus River the obligation of re-foresting those lands with cork oak and other trees. This was as well as producing timber for the royal navy. It was forbidden to cut down "cork trees, young cork trees, oaks and holm oak", which were protected wholly for the royal navy. The protection was from the River Elga, at the end of the Rosmaninhal, to Abrantes, as referred to in the Regulation of Cork Trees[44]. Cutting down the trees in these areas was punishable by whipping and two years exile. The Ordinances also dedicated special attention to encouraging the planting of olive trees[45], "worthy of recommendation (...) because of the usefulness resulting from them"[46].

Apart from establishing the rules of forestation and preservation of trees, the Ordinances forbade forest fires, punished fire-raisers with "whipping, rope hitting and street cry in villages", and forced these criminals to pay the landowners the damages caused by the flames[47]. Cattle farmers were forbidden to use burnt areas resulting from illegal fires as pastures for a year after the fire. In 1758, this punishment was extended to two years and applied to unauthorised areas of cleared land in woods and areas where fires were started on purpose. This was to prevent herdsmen from benefitting from illegally renewed pastures[48].

As to hunting, the laws in force during the reigns of D. Maria I and D. João VI were defined in the Ordinances of D. Filipe II and in the diplomas of 1612[49], 1624[50], 1776[51], and 1781[52]. Hunting small animals, like rabbit and hare, was generally allowed, with the exception of the districts of Estremadura, Alentejo and Guadiana, in which "that civil nobility degree"[53] was a prior requirement. In those regions, exceptions could be granted to the Judges of the High Court, in their properties enclosed in the royal preserves[54]. The laws of that reign also forbade the use of packs of greyhounds to chase hares in Lisbon, as this technique was an exclusive privilege of the King. The prohibition of hunting "with ammunition" was applied to all birds[55]. Partridges, in particular, could not be hunted with traps in the districts of Estremadura, Alentejo, and Guadiana[56]. With regard to hunting seasons, the law established that the activity was only allowed over adult animals and not during the breeding season[57].

The law tried to define hunting rules, as well as defending the owner against trespass by hunters and their dogs treading over fields under cultivation. The diploma from July 1st 1776 determined the prohibition of "trespass" on all cultivated fields without exception, "not only on farms, properties, vineyards, and enclosed land or long ditches, but also in all sown fields, fields with fruit on the trees, or even fields in general"[58].

This diploma also applied sanctions to hunters who invaded private property "against the will of owners, bailiffs, tenants, guards or farmhands" and determines that owners or notaries can immediately arrest trespassers who commit "the violence of entering another's property against the owner's or his representatives' will". If the trespass consisted only of entering the property with no aggression towards people or goods, the minimum penalty was three months in prison. However, if trespassers were armed and they wounded someone, the penalty meant up to ten years in the galleys or deportation to Angola, depending on whether trespassers were foot soldiers or noblemen[59]. In all other cases of crime against hunting or trespass, this diploma referred to the Ordinances of D. Filipe II.

Until 1781, the crown's laws did not define any rule regarding the hunting of large game. One can therefore conclude that outside reserves there were no restrictions on this practice. However, that same year D. Maria agreed with the suggestion of the Surveyor-General, D. Fernando José de Melo, and, by the edict of February 28th, forbade vile people from hunting noble animals (deer and wild boar). This diploma forced local authorities to follow "police law by thoroughly examining individuals who usually walk around idly", to arrest criminals, to bring actions against them, and to forward to the Police General Headquarters at the Court, all data of those who abandon "the manufacturing arts" and become hunters. "Knowing who they are, arrest them and take them to the Limoeiro prison"[60]. This legislation was in force almost in its entirety until the Constitutional Assembly, but with a variation during Junot's government in 1808.

Possession of firearms in the hands of the civil population could cause problems to the French living in Portugal. In February 1808, the French General forbade hunting with firearms, with the argument that this was a way of protecting the population from murderers. Yet, the contradiction of this argument is evident, as Acúrsio das Neves demonstrates with indignation: "Considering that, under the pretext of hunting, murders are committed daily, and that the General-in-Chief's intention is to orderly destroy hunting in those lands where it might be harming" (...) "the hunter and the road killer are put side by side, what a proportion of penalties!

(...) To destroy hunting he forbids, with the death penalty, the act of hunting: how inconsistent!"[61] Behind this protection measure was Junot's possible intention to disarm the civil population and deprive it of fighting instruments. After the French army's withdrawal in 1812, the Portuguese legislation was put into force again, the rules of hunting and forest law that had been in force until February 1808 being applied until 1821.

Apart from defining the hunting law, the Ordinances still safeguarded another kind of hunting, the capture of predators. Hunting wolves was mainly intended to protect human lives, and flocks, or herds, and to safeguard the crops from these predators[62]. That is why, unlike what happened with the game species, whose hunting was forbidden during the breeding season, one of the compulsory wolf hunts intentionally took place during that time, in order to exterminate cubs, if possible, at birth. Throughout the whole Middle and Modern Ages, the wolf was the only animal not included in the legislation regarding the general imposition of a closed season during the breeding season. Regarded as a permanent threat, this was the only species whose total extinction was encouraged. Money prizes were awarded to those who killed wolves at any time of the year[63]. The imminent danger the wolf represented, as well as the fear its presence caused, encouraged wolf hunts in the municipalities by royal imposition[64].

The legislation of 1549, which was in force until 1834, with a brief interval from 1820 to 1823, forced local elites in municipalities, donees' properties, and auditorships to hunt wolves every six months. This was also at the request of local communities, or by royal determination during periods in between. This legal disposition was to be applied unchanged across the whole kingdom, making no kind of social distinction[65]. Within the entire hunting activity, the elimination of wolves is the only circumstance in which the Crown, hunters, gamekeepers, and rural populations agree. To this end, they made great efforts, with no conflicts between the parties.

In short, the legislation in general allowed the use of forest resources by the whole population and the Crown's officers promoted the forest's development. Hunting by all individuals was allowed, though the species hunted and the hunting practices were socially differentiated. Finally, municipalities promoted the hunting of wolves as a measure of protection to local populations. As will be seen later, the hunting and forest law in reserves was substantially different from that of the general system, though it was similar in relation to the issue of eliminating predators.

1.1.3. Royal reserves

Having stated the rules regarding the kingdom's hunting and forest laws, it is now time to analyse the royal reserves system. Before starting, however, it is important to consider the geographical distribution (Picture 1).

Between 1777 and 1821, the contour of royal reserves followed a territorial line starting in Lisbon and going along three distinct axes. To the North, following the coastline until Óbidos, were the reserves of Lisbon and its surroundings, Colares, Queluz, Sintra and Óbidos. In the same direction moving further inland were the reserves of Samora Correia, Pancas, Benavente, Erra, Muja, Salvaterra de Magos, Chamusca, Almeirim and Vale de Santarém. To the South, the reserves of Arrábida, Palma and Pinheiro, and Pera e Comporta extended along the Sado estuary, beginning in Setúbal and going south until Santa Margarida do Sado.

In 1800, this map underwent some changes (Picture 2). Following the publication of the regulations of game reserves, the reserve of Almeirim was extinct, and the reserves of Muge, Benavente, Salvaterra de Magos, Samora Correia and Pinheiro were reduced; the coastline's wood reserves, as well as the reserves of Santarém and of the Sado estuary maintained their boundaries[66].

In spite of the reduction of reserved areas in 1800, one realises that, during the reigns of D. Maria I and D. João VI, the geographical space filled by royal wood and game reserves was a significant part of the kingdom. Apart from the dimension of the Crown's reserved property, royal reserves were found in privileged areas with good access by land, river and sea.

Sketch of royal reserves in 1777, 1779, 1800[67]

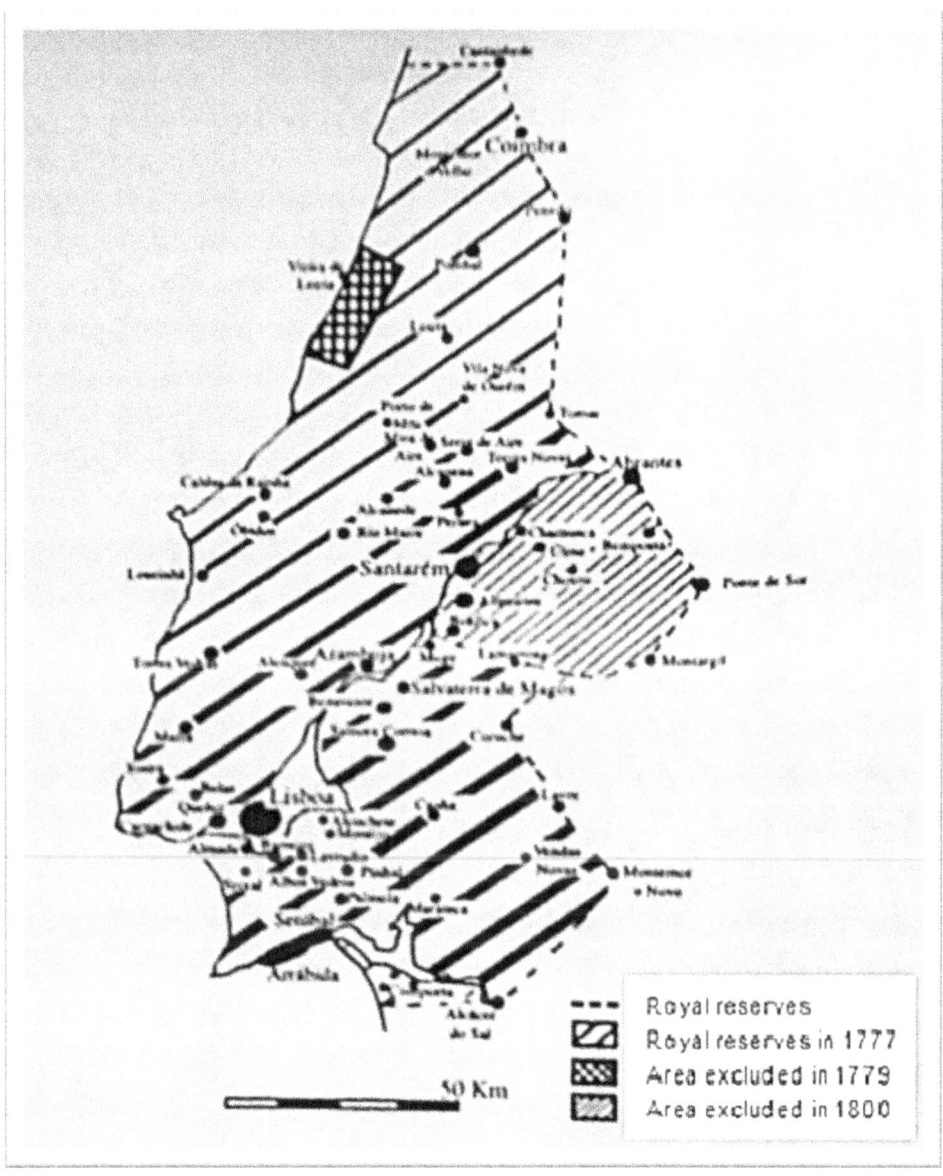

Figure 1

Sketch of royal reserves in the Portuguese territory 1777, 1779, 1800[68]

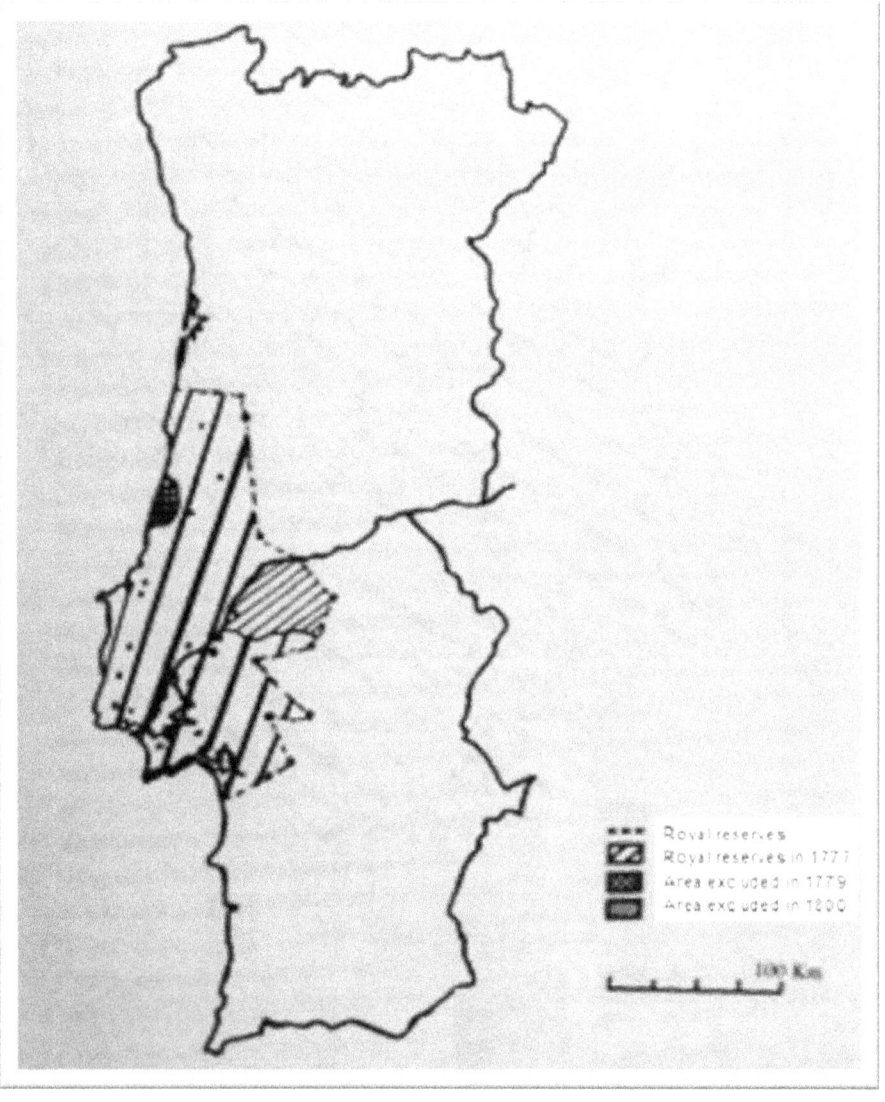

Figure 2

Adding to these features is the lands' altitude. In fact, reserves around the hydrological basins of the Tagus and Sado Rivers were located on exceptional quality arable lands, the fertile fields of the marshes. Apart from this increase in productive value, in between these rich arable areas were found dense woods, abundant in large game.

On the other hand, accessibility by waterways through the Tagus and Sado Rivers allowed the royal family to travel quickly and safely from Lisbon to the reserves and back. This way, the King's ministers and the Surveyor-General travelled easily to game reserves during the "winter journeys" of "His Majesties" to dispatch the necessary documentation[69].

The location of wood reserves, alongside game reserves, in Ribatejo and Alentejo had to do with the fact that this made the transportation of logs to naval yards easier. Originating from the pinewoods and oak plantations of the region, and profiting from the powerful river current, to transport them, these logs were sent through the Tagus River and its confluence at Lisbon and through the Sado River until Setúbal[70].

Likewise, the easiness of communication with the coastline's wood reserves north from Lisbon was guaranteed both by sea, and by the road connecting Lisbon to Coimbra. The logs from the coast were transported by sea and, from 1751 onwards, with the creation of the *Regulations of Leiria's Pinewoods*, the Lis River fulfilled the same function as the rivers located more to the south, i.e. the transportation of logs from Leiria's pinewood to the "Navy's factory"[71]. One has to bear in mind that, in spite of Leira's pinewood being the main raw material supplier to the naval construction works, there was the constant need for timber to maintain the navy and its warehouses. Allied to the late reforestation of royal pinewoods, this influenced D. Filipe II, as early as 1605, to reserve the Crown's woods and apply the reserve system to private reserves.

The excellent location of natural resources allowed for profitable results of both the economic and pleasure functions of royal reserves[72]. These features, provided the logic of the Regulations of the Surveyor-General's Department in 1605, were mostly kept until the end of the 18th century.

As noted by several authors[73], the Regulations of the Surveyor-General's Department of 1605 formally created an organisation in charge of managing all wood and game reserves of the Crown, and defined the organic law and the procedure standards of the body of officers of the

Surveyor-General's Department[74]. This implied defining command posts, constituting patrols, equipping the guards, and defining the officers' wages, according to their category. On the other hand, the document established, as referred to previously, the creation of a new position: the reserve judge[75]. This magistrate had the privilege of judging all criminal cases occurring inside reserves and listed in the Regulations of the Surveyor-General's Department.

In 1650, D. João VI proclaimed the *Regulations of the Judge of Reserves, Enclosed Arable Land, Woods and Groves of Trees*. This diploma created the post of the Reserve Judge, carried out by an Associate Justice of the *Desembargo do Paço*. This magistrate's function was to handle all Supreme Court cases related to the Surveyor-General's Department. He only answered to the Surveyor-General and to the King.

Headed by the Surveyor-General, who managed a large area of territory and disposed, with royal approval, both of a body of guards and magistrates under his command, it was by these regulations of 1650 that the Surveyor-General's Department became fully autonomous from other powers of the Ancient Regime. However, regarding the management and administration of natural resources of reserves, the Regulations of 1650 changed nothing of what was defined in 1605. From this point of view, the officers, wood and gamekeepers should not only watch over the wood and hunting grounds, but also guarantee correct forest management, and above all, condition the use of land reserved for pasture.

Forest management implied the systematic reforestation after any tree fall, and the careful selection of trees to cut down, so as not to open too large spaces in the woods, thus avoiding the destruction of its fauna's habitats[76]. This treatment of the woods was to be applied to both wood and game reserves.

Concerning pastures, the edict of May 19th 1778 forbade pasturing in royal reserves and in the reserves of the Infantado[AN]. Transgressions were punished by confiscating cattle. However, any relapse into that crime made D. Maria take measures that were more drastic. This established "life deportation to Angola if it appears that they perpetrate whatever minimal abuse every time they do not have express written licence from D. João"[77].

Apart from defining the conditions of timber allocation to the Crown, the Regulations of 1605 also established the formulae of timber concessions from the reserves, in properties belonging to the King, or in the properties of other landowners, to the population or donees.

From the beginning of the 17th century, the King interfered directly in the administration of the donees' goods. Having the exclusive right of preserving woods or withdrawing that right, the Crown prevented the allocation of timber, felling or rough-hewing, without licence from the Surveyor-General in private woods subject to the Regulations of 1605.

On the other hand, from 1758 onwards, the grant of any licence to cut down forest resources asked by donees whose woods were included in the Regulations, required royal authorisation. This might be granted following consultation with the Surveyor-General. However, even after authorisations were granted, rough-hewing could only take place if watched by the officers of the Surveyor-General's Department. As in the Crown's reserves, the guards of the woods serving the King, support and supervise the tasks to guarantee an alternate cut down of trees in order to avoid the transformation of the forest into a moor.

By imposing the absolute need of a royal authorisation for any kind of cutting down of forest resources, the Crown exercised its power over the population in general, and over the higher echelons of the kingdom. In the last quarter of the 18th century, distinguished individuals like the Surveyor-General D. Joana or the Marquis of Nisa had to submit to this rule established by the regulations of the Surveyor-General. The rule was enforced even when it concerned private properties[78]. This mechanism of interference in the management of a titleholder's properties granted institutional and *de facto* power to the Surveyor-General's Department.

This kind of interference was also felt in game reserves, where restrictions to the alienation of forest resources, and even to the use of moors, were felt even more harshly. In question was the safeguarding of habitats of game for exclusive royal use. However, the status of noble birth allowed the higher social levels in the kingdom to question the authority of the officers of the Surveyor-General's Department and to try to break the rules imposed upon reserves.

In a letter to the Surveyor-General, on September 22nd 1778, the Judge of Muja complains of knowing from the start that he can do nothing against the criminals who started a fire because they are servants to the Duke of Cadaval: "around here, aside from others, I continuously see the goats of His Excellency the D. of Cadaval and, of course, by the formality with which the referred fire was set one understands that it was set by herdsmen to create pastures for their cattle. I will investigate this matter, but I know it is useless because of my post.

This is what I communicate to the magistrate of Santarém"[79]. To restrain the unpunished actions of the nobility, the Surveyor-General interjects. In December 1782, after having been informed that the Duke of Cadaval was hunting in the royal reserve of Sintra, he proceeded to confirm that His Excellency the Duke in fact held a hunting licence from the Queen, "by the responsibilities I am obliged to, due to my post, (...) I beg your Excellency to show me the authorisation you have, so that I can fulfil the necessary duties I have"[80].

In game reserves, the King had the exclusive right to hunt large game, namely, deer and wild boar, "I hereby order & defend that no person of any state & condition will be bold enough to kill, inside the mentioned reserves, any pig, sow, piglet, or any large or small game, nor lay any kind of snare to catch game, or wish to hunt, as long as they do not kill pigs nor deer"[81].

As to minor game, the King kept to himself the exclusive right to kill partridges with firearms and forbade, in reserves south of the Tejo, any hunting of this species with pointer dogs[82]. In 1787, D. Maria reinforced this prohibition, which had proved ineffective, and ordered the killing of all dogs found in royal reserves[83]. With regard to hares, the royal exclusive of hunting them with greyhound dogs was kept in the reserves of Lisbon and Sintra[84].

Although the Regulations defined rules to apply in royal reserves, throughout the 18th century several of the proclaimed diplomas went beyond the dispositions established by the Regulations. Generally, infractions committed inside royal reserves triggered extra repressive measures, published in the legislation not included in the ordinances or sent only to Reserve Judges. These were made known to the population in general by edicts posted in villages located inside the reserves[85]. This process was frequently used by monarchs such as D. João V, D. José and D. Maria I, from 1733 onwards.

Although D. João V moved more often between Mafra and Lisbon than between Salvaterra de Magos and the capital city[86], the reserve of Salvaterra was frequently visited during his brother's, the Infante D. Francisco, winter journeys[87]. According to him, the inviolable sacred space was constantly invaded by poachers, which reduced the number of animals at the disposal of the King to exercise "royal amusement"[88]. Game species in reserves, from rabbits to deer, were constantly hunted by the lower classes. On the other hand, fires destroyed the forest where the fauna reproduced and not only killed game species themselves, but also scared away the ones that survived. In light of such shame and disrespect towards the royal person, Infante D. Francisco insisted on exemplary punishment for these high treason crimes; naturally, his voice was duly heard.

Five years after the Black Act was passed in Britain, which included poaching in the long list of crimes punished by the capital penalty[89], D. João V granted his permission for such a measure. In 1733, an edict is placed in all royal game reserves determining the application of the death penalty to all individuals caught red-handed "in the very act of hunting", who resist prison, or run away from reserve guards. In such cases, the guards were allowed to shoot to kill[90].

In 1763, "at the request the population", D. José reduced the reserved area of Arrábida, which had belonged to the House of Aveiro[91]. However, in 1771, this King guaranteed the safeguarding of a part of this reserve for his nephew, a member of the House of Aveiro and the Marquis of Pombal did, or could do, nothing to oppose him![92]

It was still during D. José's reign, in 1775, that an innovation to the patrolling of the reserve and royal woods of Almeirim and the game reserves of Santarém was introduced. The "Regulations of 1775" established that during the summer months, an army's cavalry detachment was sent to those lands. Provided with a bigger number of forces, night and day watches were organised, thus guaranteeing a continuous twenty-four-hour surveillance. Watches were kept regularly in the reserves of Almeirim, Benavente, Coruche, Muja, Pinheiro, Salvaterra, Samora and Belmonte, and Santarém.[93] To increase the efficiency of these watches, the Surveyor-General's Department was given a cartographic instrument which enabled officers to know the territory better, and have an immediate perception of the area under surveillance: the map of the game reserves of Santarém, first published in 1775[94].

If D. José had taken measures to improve the watches over the game reserves of Santarém, where the large game was hunted, and granted special attention to the reserve of Lisbon, abundant in small game, D. Maria I, on the other hand, focused her attention on the large game reserves of Ribatejo and Alentejo.

In an effort to halt the flood of poaching that had plagued royal reserves, the Queen took enforcement measures. From May 1777, D. Fernando José de Melo, recently appointed

Surveyor-General, presented the ideal response to this task and re-invigorated the management of the institution.

Assuming beforehand that everything was in a state of slackness, the Surveyor-General D. Fernando took immediate action. In May, he sent letters to all Reserve Judges, Chief Gamekeepers and Chief woodkeepers[an] imposing a new rule, i.e. making it compulsory for them to send monthly reports to the General Office of the Surveyor-General's Department reporting their activities. He also threatened all officers with sending them to prison and even firing them, in the event of negligence or connivance with crimes occurring inside reserves, thus ending all privileges to which they were entitled by their position. Furthermore, they were also to be judged by the rules established in the Regulations of the Surveyor-General's Department.

In June still, by order of the Queen and on her behalf, the Surveyor-General began a series of regular inquiries into the situation of reserves. He came to conclude that in spite of the legislation in force, both their game and forest resources were subject to plundering with impunity. Authorities were not playing their role and the mechanisms of policing were ineffective. He hired a Judge of the High Court, Diogo Inácio de Pina Manique, who came especially from the Court to run the inquiries, analyse the state of things and intervene. His methods were radical. Pina Manique arrived and imposed terror. Threats against officers of the Surveyor-General's Department passed into action and he arrested incompetent guards who abused power. He even put in jail a gamekeeper who, in the fulfilment of his duty, carried his gun loaded[95].

Of the officers who were orderly and obedient to the hierarchic chain of command, few willingly accepted the Judge of the High Court. Gamekeepers and Judges themselves now doubted to whom the command of the Department belonged; whether to the Surveyor-General, far away at the Court, or to the man with the confidence of the Queen. Hiding behind his loyalty to D. Fernando José de Melo, the judge of the reserve of Santarém refused to execute an order from Pina Manique, appealing to the Surveyor-General to help him clarify the procedure he should follow[96]. D. Fernando's answer is unequivocal: he has full trust in Manique and all reserve officers must obey him[97].

The Surveyor-General granted Pina Manique all the necessary powers to act in reserves on his and the Queen's behalf[98]. With full jurisdiction over all magistrates and officers of the game and wood reserves, except over the Surveyor-General, Pina Manique restructured the reserve patrols. He included herdsmen and shepherds in the body of guards, forcing them to watch over the woods during the summer months and making them criminally responsible for any fires occurring during their watch shifts[99]. This measure was intended to put an end to forest fires. However, in August 1778, answering the actions of the magistrate, the frequency of forest fires increased, from one every three days to one every day, and were set simultaneously in several places of the same reserve. The measures as described above only had full effect in the following summer.

In 1779, a diploma from 1752 was restored, imposing on shepherds who had set fires in the woods the prohibition against use of the pastures for two years after the fire had been set. Both diplomas from 1612 and 1614, forbidding hunting with firearms in royal reserves, were restored. In spite of constituting the legal expression of the restrictions imposed on the use of reserve resources, they had in fact become obsolete during the 17th and 18th centuries, not being applied at all[100]. When D. Maria ordered the Judge of Aldeia Galega to run an inquiry and arrest all firearm holders, he could not fulfil her wish. There were more armed men than space inside prisons and the law forbidding the possession of weapons had become obsolete[101]. Other measures had to be taken. The first was to inform and order all villagers living inside royal reserves, with no retaliation whatsoever, that they should return their weapons, emphasizing the prohibition of firearm possession. After they had "voluntarily" given their weapons back, searches and arrests were possible. Otherwise, the Judge would have to detain entire villages. Nevertheless, the problem of lack of space in prisons still existed[102]. In sight of such evidence, the Surveyor-General yielded and once again, in June 1779, published an edict renewing the prohibition of firearm possession inside royal reserves, before starting to chase poachers and put them in prison.

These measures, as well as the application of the new surveillance regulations of the reserve of Almeirim (1775) and of Pina Manique on the patrolling of reserves, had a long-term effect. It was hard to impose, since reserve judges and gamekeepers were "very glad" about the appointment of the Surveyor-General. However, they were "confused" by the determinations of "Judge Manique"[103].

During the decades of seventeen eighty and seventeen ninety, an effort was made to tighten the surveillance. However, this proved itself ineffective, and crimes against royal reserves were practised regularly, either by officers of the Surveyor-General's Department, who negotiated the resources as though they belonged to them, or by poachers and woodcutters. With regard to timber traffic, it was more frequent in the reserves of Samora Correia, Pera e Comporta, and Óbidos, since these supplied great quantities of timber to the Court, and for the construction of ships.

In the first reserves mentioned, the network of complicities constituted a relatively complex system, which will be dealt with in Chapter 4. In Óbidos, the fact that the King was not present and the physical distance from Court guaranteed a larger impunity to crime and made it easier for the chain of corruption to develop. Bailiffs eliminated any record of complaints made by the inhabitants of that reserve, and gamekeepers were bribed to grant licences to cut down wood in the enclosed woods of the Regulations[104]. Regarding poaching, officers also practised it regularly, from the reserve of Sintra to the one of Santarém, as we shall see.

In 1796, in face of this situation, the Surveyor-General suggested that Prince D. João change reserve regulations[105]. In practice, this system made soil cultivation impracticable, since it imposed too many restrictions on the use of land. The growing pressure from the population also demanded the occupation of those areas. On the other hand, crimes against the forest and the animals occurred too often, and the Surveyor-General's Department no longer had means to prevent them. Furthermore, the Prince Regent and the Court mainly used the game reserves of Lisbon, Sintra, Belas, Mafra, Samora, Benavente, Muge and Erra, and Salvaterra[106]. In face of this diagnosis, in a letter from August 8th 1796[107], he suggested the reduction of reserved areas and the conversion of grounds there into arable land. In the same letter, the Surveyor-General presented a very dark perspective of the situation of royal reserves and listed the existing problems:

"Madam – Experience has shown that the royal reserves of the South are constantly being attacked, both by those who take an interest in agriculture and farming, and by thieves who continually infest them. The first ones incessantly criticise the way the land is being occupied, maliciously setting snares to lead to the extinction of game who damage their sown fields; the latter poach royal reserves in search of profit from the game they kill, audaciously defying the guards and making it thus impossible to go around without carrying a sword. The extension of the grounds enclosed no doubt gives reason to the complaints of the first ones and makes it more difficult to prevent the insults of the latter. Therefore, it seemed convenient to suggest some measures to Your Majesty that would useful in the search of a solution to both cases.

"Your Majesty's royal intention being that of favouring agriculture, as long as it is compatible with the State's interest in the plantation and preservation of timber for the Royal Navy, and with the privileges held by the Kings of these kingdoms and the Sovereigns of the most illustrious nations, which implies the enclosing of land for their amusement, Your Majesty will be asked to limit and reduce the extension of the referred reserves, with no change whatsoever to the Department."[108]

D. Francisco da Cunha presented solutions for the disrespected reserves subject to and to satisfy the pressure to occupy part of the reserved grounds. Regarding economic development, the Regulations of 1796 reflected the practical application of the physiocratic creed of the Royal Academy of Sciences: agricultural development in Portugal was possible, necessary and urgent. The extinction of some game reserves and their immediate conversion to agriculture represented a first attempt of the Crown to promote agricultural development. This attempt was prior to the publication of the 1810 tithe decree and the decree granting special privileges to the growing of cereal, of April 15th 1815.

The most important measures concerned the reduction of game reserve areas and the transformation of uncultivated grounds in those reserves into spaces of agricultural undertaking. Besides, the Surveyor-General suggests the inclusion of the reserve of Pancas in royal reserves: "from this reserve originates much of the damage to royal reserves / apart from causing deformity / since thieves, after being whipped inside it, easily pass into other royal reserves"[109]. Furthermore, "because of its closeness to the Court it is very much adequate to Your Majesty's daily amusement, and it would be very convenient that it was included inside royal reserves, exclusively in what regards hunting"[110]. As to forest resources management the Surveyor-General suggested that the reserve of Pancas should carry on being managed by its landlord, "in what concerns timber and the woods, its landlord would maintain the right to use them freely"[111].

Apart from trying to answer to "those who take an interest in agriculture and farming" with these measures and thus safeguarding resources, the Surveyor-General was concerned with the preservation of game species, showing that "the motive that takes thieves to invade reserves is the profit they can get from the sale of meat and fur"[112]. He therefore suggested that His Majesty could reduce the crime wave by forbidding "any person to buy those furs and meat or allowing the sale in their house, harshly punishing those who have bought anything visibly stolen or have kept stolen objects in their houses. The whole negotiation process or the use of animals from that district and fifteen miles around was to be considered a vice. Also, the value of each animal should always be higher than the value of a silver coin"[113]. Exception should be made to "the animals killed during royal hunts, whose fur and meat can be used"[114]. However, the Reserve Judge has to verify whether these have been legally hunted and give each hunter a "ticket declaring the legitimate and non-illegal acquisition of those animals"[115].

In this same document, the Surveyor-General suggested an original measure in order to more easily catch these criminals, be they hunters or dealers who trade or treat animals illegally hunted inside reserves. He wished to "give them the same fines as those applied to promoters, stolen-goods dealers, and masters and officers of tanning factories, if they received the aforementioned skins within a fifteen mile area to tan them. Authorities in those places can, whenever they find it appropriate, proceed to search inside those factories and examine their registers in order to know who the transgressors are"[116].

With regard to weapons he announced new measures to restrain the use of firearms and defined that "No person of any kind or condition whatsoever / apart from reserve officers / can hold any gun in their house or outside it, not only within the limits of the new royal reserves but also five miles away from them. Whoever does so will be considered a poacher and be punished accordingly. Exception is made to those who, simply passing by, carry their guns with no gunlock"[117].

Going further in his presentation of measures to simultaneously safeguard cultures and prevent royal game from being wounded, the Surveyor-General believed in the prohibition of "all nets to protect wheat-fields; those can only be used when they are put around sown fields and in fact do protect the fruits, but do not serve as snares to catch the reserve's game"[118].

Regarding pasturing, D. Francisco da Cunha suggested the introduction of conditions that eased the use of bushes in royal reserves. "Cattle keepers who inhabit the new reserved spaces can legally enter those bushes with their cattle, as long as no fires occur in them; this being the case, they are deprived of this prerogative and will be considered fire-raisers; in the case of their innocence, after the real guilty person is put in prison, they will be released"[119].

In order to safeguard hunting conditions, the Surveyor-General suggested that dense woods be eliminated and bushes be burnt to create pastures destined for royal game, "Your Majesty should order, by the edict of May 29th 1779, that the bushes considered adequate be burnt for pastures, so that they can be used by royal game and by royal cattle". This placed the living conditions of the animals ahead of those of the local people[120].

In the same text, he tried to end to another problem, the use of dogs by peasants who hunted inside reserves, stating that "common dogs or any kind of watch-dog" should be allowed, whereas "all other dogs which abusively enter reserves originate the destruction of all game inside the reserve"[121] and should therefore be forbidden.

As to vigilance, D. Francisco da Cunha suggested that "the 1775 Plan should be entirely kept at game and wood reserves, as this watch method was the best for firefighting, a terrible problem in reserves"[122]. To put these measures into practice the Surveyor-General suggested a change in the reserves' judicial system so that the monopoly of crime cases occurring inside royal reserves was taken from the hands of reserve judges, and "the jurisdiction of reserve judges is cumulative with territorial judges, allowing them all not only to act against all transgressors by own motion and summarily"[123]. They should also be allowed "to receive accusations in secret". Territorial judges were forced to inquire about these articles and those of the Regulations in General Inquiries. Whenever these judges and reserve judges inquired simultaneously on the same crime, the crime was presented to the jurisdiction by the one who first arrested the criminal, "mandating the guilt through a commission to the other court, which will certainly be sent back to him"[124].

After having stated the defence's case and the penalties for transgressors, the Surveyor-General presented promotion and economic development measures for reserves. Given the shortage of timber, especially in wood reserves, it was the Surveyor-General himself who suggested to the Prince Regent that he should order the reforestation of dilapidated spaces, "In conclusion, the future urgent need for timber and wood being taken care of, it would be very useful if Your Majesty would order royal and wood reserves to plant at least pinewoods in sites and lands naturally unsuitable for any other kind of plantation"[125]. As a reference, he presented the measure another King had taken 100 years before, "proceeding as King D. Pedro II had already done in the year 1699, when he had a box of northern stone pine seeds sent to the Surveyor-General Francisco de Melo, with a warning of October 30th of that same year, for him to plant them in the most appropriate places and locations"[126].

At the end of this list of suggested changes to the Regulations in force since the 17th century, the Surveyor-General adds a note saying that all these measures should be supported by "a licence working as an act of law, known by everybody and that nobody could say they have ignored its existence"[127].

His suggestions would only take effect years after, in the Regulations of March 21st 1800, which follow the original proposals almost completely. The new regulations eased the performance of the Surveyor-General and the Surveyor-General's Department, and helped achieve more effective action by agents in the territory. This in part because of the reduction of the reserved areas and perhaps due to increased policing. Assigning territorial judges to criminal cases which occurred inside the reserves and brought a new dynamism to the application of justice thus contributing to concentrate efforts on a better management and protection of reserves. However, this also ended the jurisdictional autonomy that reserves had enjoyed since 1605.

Yet, the creation of a specific system for game reserves, as with the Regulations of 1800, in force at the same time as another system regarding exclusively wood reserves, generated huge confusion in the interpretation of the law. Most territorial authorities of municipalities with woods defined by the Regulations of 1605, as Óbidos, Leiria, Benavente and Samora Correia, interpreted the new regulations as extensible to all royal reserves, thus triggering jurisdiction conflicts among reserve judges and municipality judges. During the years 1800 and 1801, the biggest confusion was around the definition of each body's competences. Nevertheless, essentially and in all reserves not mentioned in the diploma of March 21st 1800, the Surveyor-General's Department followed the Regulations of 1605.

The clarification of the new regulations' contents came with the decree of August 18th 1801, in which the Prince granted the payment of an extra salary to officers deprived of their offices: "and stating that only the posts of those reserves listed in the referred licence [1800] are exclusively part of my royal providence; in no way are the ones of other reserves not mentioned there; these should be kept and run as they were before its publication, and with the same wages for those officers"[128].

The reserves of Almeirim, Chamusca and Santarém north of the Tejo having been made extinct, the judges' posts of those reserves became extinct in 1800, as well as the judges' posts of the game reserves that remained as such: Samora Correia, Pancas, Pera e Comporta, Benavente, Muge, Salvaterra de Magos, and Santarém. In wood reserves, all the posts and offices were kept according to the Regulations of 1605. In 1801, the supremacy of the Surveyor-General over all royal game and wood reserves defined by the Regulations of 1605, except for the pinewoods of Leiria, was also confirmed. The Surveyor-General was enabled to appoint wolf hunters in all districts of the kingdom and to all officers of the Surveyor-General's Department. Therefore, until the French invasion, the diplomas of 1800 and 1801 were in force in game reserves. The diploma of 1605 and the one of 1758 redefined, in wood reserves, the use of pastures and wood felling.

As to game legislation, the Regulations of 1800 introduced a significant change to the previous legislation. For the first time, a non-noble individual could hunt deer or fallow deer in royal reserves as long as he had a licence from the reserve's keeper and was accompanied by him. Having caught the animals, he must take their skins to the reserve's tanning master for him to treat them in his store. Although still with social restrictions and connected to a specific economic activity, the hunt of noble animals by some individuals of the lower social classes shows the pressure put upon this resource, and the sustenance needs felt at the time. Once again, the law ratified common practice.

With the French invasions, however, the situation changed. In a letter from March 12th 1808, by order of Junot, D. Pedro is informed that the post of Surveyor-General no longer exists, being replaced by the post of *Inspecteur de Parcs et Forêts Réservés.* On the 28th of that same month, L'Oison presents the Regulations of Forests and Reserved Parks to D. Pedro:

"1ᵉʳ – que vos fonctions consistent seulement dans l'inspection sur les forêts et parcs réserves tant pour la conservation de la chasse que pour celle des bois ; 2ᵉᵐᵉ que vous **devait** prendre la qualité d'Inspecteur des forêts et parcs réservés ; 3ᵉᵐᵉ que les gardes des forêts patrouillés peuvent continuer de porter de l'habit vert qui indique leur caractère ; 4ᵉᵐᵉ que le Dezembargador Juiz Geral, Dezembargador Fiscal, le secrétaire et autres employés non supprimés doivent continuer leurs fonctions ; 5ᵉᵐᵉ qu'il a été donné des ordres de disposer, comme on voudrait, des faucons de l'établissement à Salvaterra"[129].

Thus, this diploma declared that the Surveyor-General's functions only consisted of the surveillance of wood and game reserves, as well as in guaranteeing the preservation of these resources. It also determined that, from that moment on, the General Inspector of Reserves must take the post under the title Inspector of Woods and Forests; that reserve guards can go on using the same green outfits that indicate their function. The post of General Associate Justice of Reserves was kept, and the Royal Falconry of Salvaterra de Magos remained as it was.[130].

The French government's strategy revealed intelligence and probably meant to pass the idea that Junot respected national institutions. Following a line of continuity in keeping a paramilitary and judicial body, this message could be transmitted through an authority know to the population and using Portuguese uniforms. However, though the French Council found an apparent co-operation strategy with the Surveyor-General's Department's authorities, maintaining the administrative and judicial authorities, it withdrew *de facto* authority and manoeuvre space of the Surveyor-General. The General Inspector of Forests and Reserves was now a mere pawn that carried out orders issued by the French government[131].

By maintaining a Portuguese policing body to which the population was already used to, though they did not respect them, Junot avoided another outcry against the replacement of heads in national institutions. Anyhow, the number of effects on duty did not compromise the French army's authority, especially after authorisation to carry firearms had been withdrawn from the keepers. In 1809, with the departure of Junot's troops from Portugal, the Surveyor-General took back his post and the diplomas of 1800 and 1605 were in force again until the Constitutional Assembly.

In spite of the re-establishment of Portuguese legislation, the management of reserves remained weakened. With the clear autonomy chief keepers held in the areas under their jurisdiction, reserves were now managed by these officers as though they were Crown donees. They took care of these properties, leased farmlands and imposed taxes upon the population for their own profit, as happened with the judge of the reserve of Sintra, who administered it as though it was his own[132]. Besides, from the end of 1808 onwards, the population was armed with firearms to fight the "invaders". They naturally began using that equipment for their own profit when hunting, keeping it after the Invasions were over. The Surveyor-General D. Pedro complains about this fact to Prince D. João, justifying his incapacity to police reserves. In reply to the Prince Regent's indignation, as he could not understand how in a plundered country there were no conditions to keep reserves protected, D. Pedro da Cunha reports his difficulties, and the fact that many firearms given to civilians had not been returned[133]. However, D. João doubted that.

Policing and preserving the Surveyor-General's Department became hopelessly impracticable. In Brazil, the Prince worried about the partridges that did not arrive alive at the Court in Rio de Janeiro and so prevented him from amusing himself by hunting. The Prince questioned the performance of the acting Surveyor-General. Feeling insulted, harmed, and sad because of the harsh words and the suspicion his lord showed towards him, D. Pedro invoked honour and appealed to his father. This last appeal was more effective[134].

D. Francisco José de Melo, Surveyor-General, Officer of the Royal House, Governor of Arms of Alentejo and the Algarve, head of the insurrection against the French, pledged his word. D. Pedro's father pacified the royal invective, converting it into praise to the performance of the acting Surveyor-General. However, the King took the opportunity to remind him that above all D. Pedro da Cunha must protect reserves... to guarantee the regular supply of partridges destined for Rio de Janeiro.

From 1809 to 1812, the letters exchanged between D. Pedro and the Prince Regent dealt mainly with the very important matter of raising and sending partridges to Brazil. In addition, they occasionally addressed the management of the Surveyor-General's Department[135].

From 1812 onwards, the monarch sent some diplomas from Rio de Janeiro with the intention of reorganising the Surveyor-General's Department and safeguarding reserved spaces, and once again the Surveyor-General carried out investigations. These resulted in several criminal procedures, mainly against members of the Department's hierarchy[136].

Although the King held exclusive access to resources in royal reserves, this rigidity ended up broken. This was on the one hand, through licences granted to the people, to Department officers, to neighbouring reserve judges and municipality magistrates, and to titled nobility, as well as through other resources, such as pastures and wood. On the other hand, it was through crimes committed against reserves.

1.2. The Liberal Revolution: disruption or continuity?

On January 30th 1821, the Constitutional Assembly began and the following February 8th, the congress resulting from the Revolution extinguished royal game reserves. The act for the abolition of seigniorial rights, so very much hated, was only proclaimed a month later, on April 7th. This swiftness in abolishing royal reserves, a fact largely overlooked, reveals by itself the importance these had for the rural society.

In 1821, the petition sent to the Constitutional Assembly by the inhabitants of Cantanhede explained how the people of the reserved lands of the Marquis of Marialva were shocked, "an extensive reserve in which there is the most severe and strict prohibition to hunt, cut down wood and make charcoal, in which the poor inhabitants see themselves not only deprived of the freedom of going to their farms with a rifle but also forced to necessarily suffer the damage in sown and wheat fields caused by birds and wild harmful animals, which reproduce themselves so abundantly because of that prohibition. Those, my lord, are the poignant evils that turn sad and miserable the condition of more than ten thousand inhabitants of which this reserve is composed"[137].

In a similar record, the petitions of Palmela and Montemor-o-Novo clearly show the abuses committed on the population by tenants who imposed the reserve system abolished by the Constitutional Assembly, "Your Majesty having so wisely extinguished reserves, since they were so harmful to agriculture, it looks as though this attitude should really put an end to them;

however, this was not the case, because the attitude prevails and, what is even worse, the abuse also prevails, because tenants do not want to know whether the land is inside or outside the reserve's limit and fine people at their own will"[138]. Some landlords of religious orders, like the Friars of Macieira do Dão, also oppressed inhabitants with reserve system's laws, making it difficult for them to use moors and forests, and giving peasants no access to hunting in the barren lands of their properties.[139]

To find a solution for this problem, members of parliament debated the issue and acted promptly. Discussion in parliament was brief and in two sessions only, on January 31st and on February 7th, the matter was settled. The main speaker on this issue, Borges de Carneiro, presented the situation clearly and terribly, "The exclusive privilege of hunting and fishing is the last seed of seigniorial oppression. (…) Reserves represent a terrible and oppressive abuse against farmers. Because of this, donees have the pernicious right of having harvests destroyed, leaving inhabitants no possibility of defence".

Adding to the "vexations" the reserve system imposed to populations, they felt orphans of the royal presence. Since the King's departure to Brazil, the people of Aldeia Galega and Salvaterra de Magos had stopped feeling "favoured with the presence" of the royal family, and, adding to the pain felt because of the King's absence, populations also suffered all the restrictions imposed on villages close to the royal residence.

On the other hand, what reason justified that a poor peasant should be convicted to ten years in the galleys for having killed a deer that was destroying his means of survival? What gave someone the right to take possession of wild resources, such as water and the air, which belonged to no one? No one had that right, and no one was granted that right, "no man in the universe has property over wild animals he has not bought or reared, and over which he exercises no authority whatsoever"[140]. With the argument of private property defence, Borges de Carneiro proclaims that "all reserves should be extinguished", exceptions being made to "royal parks or any private park, as long as they are an individual property and are surrounded by walls"[141].

If the King had the legitimate right to exercise "the royal sports", this should be done in a way as not to harm someone else's property. Following this recommendation, the Royal Parks of Ajuda, Alcântara, Belém, Necessidades, and Mafra remained intact[142]. All other game reserves of the Crown were extinguished.

Safeguarding the hunting right to all citizens, the dispositions on hunting and closed seasons, as well as the supremacy of private property announced by Pombal and forbidding armed hunters to enter enclosed or sown lands, were retained. The Constitutional Assembly did not interfere with hunting law, unlike the reserve system. With the extinction of this system, the Constitutional Assembly took one further step towards the reinforcement of property rights. The conquest of the hunting right as an individual right only ended in 1867, with the first Portuguese Code of Civil Law.

However, the issue of reserves went back to parliament when local communities began to invade the National Woods. With the extinction of royal reserves in February, the State had taken into its own hands the duty of managing forests. However, since an end had been put to the Surveyor-General's Department, the National Woods were now unprotected and at the mercy of the whole population.

At the discussion of the project to extinguish the chief keepers, in the session of August 18th 1821, the need to reserve forests was re-stated. Parliament member Trigoso called to the attention of parliament the fact that State woods were in a disastrous condition: "When Congress extinguished reserves it forgot to provide for the preservation of woods"... and this situation had been going on for six months already!

However, parliamentary members believed woods, as a strategic element, should be defended. In the whole debate, this is the only point where "Misters" Trigoso, Pessanha, Borges Carneiro, Girão, Moura, Pinheiro de Azevedo, Bettencourt, and Brito agreed. In what concerned the institutional model, however, there were disagreements: some proclaimed the defence of woods through an institution supervised by the State, whilst others wished to reinforce the powers of municipalities and grant them the management of National Woods.

The fundamental issue debated here, on the question of the extinction of keepers and the defence of woods, focussed on the transfer of more estates and competences from keepers to municipalities. This was the main point of disagreement. As Mr Girão stated, "the preservation of woods is the most important issue; however, it does not depend on keepers, because they are not responsible for it; municipalities are the ones responsible for the surveillance of woods and barren grounds, according to their regulations"[143].

Parliament member Mr Girão also turned against the existence and oppression of those "men who are only there to torment the people and enjoy great privileges, as not having to pay the tax over their lands". Besides this accusation, he considered them to be true parasites whose existence was unjustified since "they make absolutely nothing, and the task of killing wolves was probably given to them with the single purpose of giving them something with which to entertain themselves". To reinforce this position, Mr Brito reacted vehemently against the illegitimacy of a chief keeper having the possibility of acted against private property and the right to use its goods, "because no one can be the judge of the twigs that will be cut down except for their own owner, as he is the only judge of his own interests"[144].

In opposition to the statements assumed in favour of the reinforcement of municipalities' competences, Trigoso (de Aragão Morato), Borges Carneiro, and Bettencourt were in favour of the maintenance of chief and under keepers to guard the National Woods, as well as the maintenance of the post of Surveyor-General of His Majesty's Woods and Forests. Trigoso even doubts the municipalities' capacity to fulfil the task of preserving forests, stating at the end of his communication: "I believe our woods are much deteriorated, but I believe they will be even worse or be lost for good if they are put in the hands of municipalities"[145].

After this debate, the issue was put to the vote and the side defending the extinction of chief keepers and the transfer of functions from the Surveyor-General's Department to municipalities won. On August 18th 1821, the decree extinguishing the post of Surveyor-General of His Majesty's Woods and Forests (although maintaining the office at the Royal House), and declaring that all officers of the Surveyor-General's Department, as well as "all tasks belonging to those offices to the present day will be returned to municipalities in the corresponding districts; these will scrupulously supervise, under the strictest responsibility, the preservation of national woods which are not under private management"[146]. Thus, an institution created in 1521 came to an end.

Applying the law of the Constitutional Assembly was a complicated and not at all peaceful process. Between February and July 1821, the Surveyor-General's Department collapsed under the chaos and confusion about competences and hierarchies. Completely disoriented, reserve judges, chief, and under keepers did not know after all whom they should obey, and wanted the Surveyor-General to clarify the situation.

Officially, from August 1821 onwards, the Surveyor-General's Department office was terminated, as can be seen by the absence of records in the record book of transgressions, only reintroduced after the counter-revolution in 1824. However, the letters sent to the Surveyor-General by his officers, showed they did not accept the new situation peacefully.

Curiously enough, the argument of giving more value to private property when safeguarding the royal parks, withdrew power from the Crown. Now it was the Parliament, which granted nobility a place to hunt, and was able to impose conditions. This assembly was the one that represented the nation, and both limited and defined leisure places destined for the King. Thus it inverted what until then had been a royal right over the entire population: the right to establish reserves.

Nevertheless, this revolutionary idyll suffers a setback after the Counter-revolution. In 1823, the Surveyor-General's Department was restored informally, recovering its position on June 5th 1824. This day, D. João VI fully restored the Regulations of 1800 on game reserves. On the other hand, wood reserves, defined by the Constitutional Assembly as "National Woods", were given back to the Crown and a department called "General Board of the Woods" was established[147].

The legislation on the management of Crown woods, having been reformulated by the regulations of National Woods, and the regulations on game reserves having been restored from 1824 onwards, were the diplomas kept in force even during the period of D. Miguel. The final extinction of the Surveyor-General's Department was in 1834, following the definite end of the Ancient Regime and the triumph of Constitutional Liberalism. In 1835, the Companhia das Lezírias "banished" the royal family from the historical space of leisure of the absolutist monarchy.

2. RESOURCE MANAGEMENT: AGRARIAN AND HUNTING EXPLOITATION

The preservation of royal reserves implied managing the tension between maintaining the *status quo* of the territory occupied by wild resources (forest and hunting), generated by the forest itself, and the "conquest" of that same territory for agricultural production and cattle rearing. Maintaining the balance or managing the conflict between two different areas of economic exploitation and use required the application of several simultaneous protection and exploitation policies. The protection of reserved spaces was achieved through the policing of reserves by officers of the Surveyor-General's Department and by jointly holding producers and users responsible for the areas used. Economic exploitation was realised through the gathering of wild goods, although in a very controlled way, and through agriculture and cattle rearing, which developed in some reserved areas.

Mixing these elements, i.e. the preservation of the "nucleus" of reserves, their "wild" part and their "human" part, was the object of natural resources' management policies, a task of the Surveyor-General. His role consisted of keeping and simultaneously valuing the natural property of the royal forests and game parks, resources that satisfied three direct needs for the Crown. These were, the King's leisure, and both the maintenance of the army and survival of rural populations.

Analysis of the constitution of the several locations composing reserves, whether game or wood reserves, ways of granting resource exploitation and use, management policies and administration of multiple-use spaces, are considered in this chapter. The way the management of royal reserves interfered in the social order of the Ancient Regime is taken into account.

2.1. Royal reserves: "wild" space and "tamed" space

The need to legislate in order to condition human acts and the consequent transformation of landscapes through the replacement of wild species by conditioned, intentionally grown species, reveals a double dimension of space in royal reserves. One of these is connected to the maximisation of resource preservation; another is connected to the transformation of spaces due to an economic activity. This was portrayed in land exploitation for agriculture, the use of moors for pasturing, the creation of pastures, and the gathering and cutting of copses and timber for diverse purposes. The reserves' tendency to naturally create and generate fauna and flora with no defined human intervention or seed and plant selection was thus transformed. Reserves became a mixed space that included wild disorderly resources and "tamed" ones. In certain reserved areas, man intervened by conditioning the growth and natural expansion of the forest and by introducing new cultures. This way, the reserve limits and conditions the geographical expansion of both spaces: the "wild" and the "tamed".

The preservation of existing resources and the exploitation of the ground have different expressions both in royal game and wood reserves. In the first ones, the preservation of wild spaces, characterised by dense and abundant vegetation that makes an area impenetrable and allows the development of game fauna, is the *raison d'être* for the reserve's existence. In wood reserves, on the other hand, the purpose is to maintain inaccessible the areas with big high trees with large diameter trunks, whose logs are appropriate for the royal navy. In these spaces, agricultural exploitation of the land where trees of "real interest" grow is denied. However, the ground is cleared, as are the different shrub layers that might encourage fires, prevent trees destined for timber from growing, and "encourage" illegal clearing up of land by intentional fire setting. In some cases, with the cleaning of forest debris, such as dried pine needles or branches that suffocate trees and make it difficult for them to grow, wood reserves are more subject to human intervention than game reserves.

Given the high number of restrictions imposed upon game reserves, in comparison to wood ones, the pressure of agriculture and pasturing on the forest was felt more strongly in the first ones than the second. In game reserves, fires intentionally set through the year, and land clearance for agriculture and charcoal production, reflect such strong pressure from human intervention. This was even after the application of the regulations of 1800. In wood reserves, the conquest of wild spaces generated land for agriculture and charcoal production sites.

Both types of reserve developed from a "centre" that one wished to maintain with specific development characteristics, inaccessible to undifferentiated free use, the exception made for the King. The reserve's centre consisted in the nucleus of the specific most important resources to be protected, and not in a geometrical centre.

Some geographers, Von Thünen, Hoyt and Burguess[148], have defined a model for the use of space that develops circles starting at the urban area and growing towards the forest. Likewise, reserves also have a "model" of exploitation and use conditioned by the protection of the forest's spot. The reserve develops in the opposite sense of towns, privileging impenetrable and unfarmed land, and trying to push farmed areas to its boundaries. At the "centre" of the reserve lies the dense wood, where agriculture and pasturing are strictly forbidden; from the "centre" to the periphery, as the woods' spot is reduced and the forest's richness decreases, licences for felling and pasturing are granted. The "centre" or the several "centres" correspond to areas of trees, destined for timber for the Crown, or areas of woods destined to grow royal game, whether they are in royal estates or private ones.

The leadership of economic activities that develop inside reserves follows an exploitation plan controlled by the Surveyor-General's Department. For this plan to be executed some rules are established regarding the use of farmlands, pastures, timber, trees' branches, shrubs and wood lying on the ground. These rules mark and limit the peasants' access to reserves.

The effectiveness in reducing the impact of damage caused against royal reserves depends on the performance of the Surveyor-Generals, of royal determinations, of the King's interest in reserves, and of political and economic internal and external conjunctures, with a direct impact on management policies, as will be analysed in Points 3.3 and 3.4.

2.2. Contracts and licences

With regard to the agrarian exploitation system in royal reserves one has to take the farmers' and the Surveyor-General's Department's interests into account. The first try to safeguard everlasting and lifelong ways of survival in the places where they live. The Surveyor-General's Department, on the other hand, looked to maintain the reserves' most sensitive areas free from agrarian exploitation and cattle rearing, trying to limit as much as possible the advancement of land clearing. Both parties wished to safeguard the land's exploitation system that mostly benefited their interests and within the law.

Fee-farm contracts and leases were two ways of allowing land exploitation. As the pressure of agriculture on reserves grows the grant of fee-farm contracts decreases. It finally ended from 1800 onwards, after the reduction of reserves. In practice, fee-farm contracts were a way of alienating reserves' assets. On the opposite side, lease contracts allowed the Crown to retrieve the lands, whether to farm them or for reforestation. The grant of royal pastures or unfarmed lands was made for limited periods. By the end of the contract, the Surveyor-General's Department did not have the obligation of renewing it. It had the possibility of profiting from the improvements made with the recovery of woods.

If the Crown tried to protect reserves from excessive agrarian exploitation, its inhabitants developed specific strategies to obtain lease contracts for those lands. As reserves suffered from the destruction of trees, farmers appealed to the Surveyor-General for land parcels where they could plant and treat trees, and requested permission to farm those lands, thus valuing the royal woods.

In 1791, Geraldo Wencislau Braancamp de Almeida Castelo-Branco was successful in such a request. The petition sent to the Surveyor-General requesting permission to farm a land in the reserve of Almeirim was granted. His arguments were "as these woods are intersected, due to several fires that arose here, the petitioner commits to protecting them until they are useful for Your Majesty's royal amusement"[149].

Wishing to be granted land for agriculture, farmers used another argument. They referred to the uselessness of trees for royal service and the lack of "bushes appropriate for game to hide", or saying that the existing woods "have no branches or timber worthy of the royal service (...), since several thick twigs (...) are rickety, and most of the thinner ones are twisted and lack quality"[150].

Fee-farm and lease contracts were established according to the activities tied to land exploitation, and demanding a relatively long stay of the farmer on the land. On the other hand, licences granted for forest gathering resources' (like timber, stumps, and charcoal) only included the period necessary for that gathering, for clearing the ground by fire or for producing charcoal.

To avoid abuse, the areas requested for agrarian exploitation were verified *in loco* by officers of the Surveyor-General's Department. Inspections of the lands were made prior to granting licences to cut down wood for the royal navy, wood and stumps for the royal house, and shrubs, twigs from the floor, stumps and branches for the peasants' domestic use and to produce charcoal.

Requests to clear the ground by fire, to improve farmlands in areas where the forest area had no importance for reserves, hid the petitioners' real intentions. These were to obtain a licence to clear the ground by fire and, under the pretext of that licence, burn the bushes and trees of those grounds to produce charcoal. After having extracted this product, they would abandon that field without ever putting into practice their "native passion" for agriculture, as happened to Joaquim Campos, inhabitant of the reserve of Óbidos.

In 1802, this tenant in fee and charcoal dealer requested a licence to clear a ground by fire in order to plant and to sow that land, supporting his arguments with the lack of capacity for forestation of the area requested. The Surveyor-General suspected this situation to be a fraud: In 1788, Joaquim Campos had already tried to fool the Department saying the land he wished to clear did not belong to the reserve. The Surveyor-General ordered "a strict and precise examination" of the land the tenant in fee was requesting for that purpose[151].

Licences for lime, brick, and tile kilns were granted mainly in Sintra, and the majority of the products were destined to maintain the royal house ("for the palace repair works"). Some requests were also made in Salvaterra de Magos, Coruche, Benavente, Chamusca and Erra. Lime produced was, in some cases, even the product the tenant in fee had to use to pay the King, as can be seen in the licence granted to António Francisco from the place of Laranja, and Manuel Nunes, living in Cascais, "to help pay the rents"[152].

2.3. Evolution of reserve management

2.3.1. Farming and forest resources

Taking over the reins of the Surveyor-General's Department at the beginning of D. Maria I's reign, and occupying the post until his death in 1787, D. Fernando José de Melo[153] profited from a peaceful period in terms of politics and economics, and eased by the continuity with which Her Majesty goes to royal reserves. "On her stays in Salvaterra, where she went every winter, from middle December until middle February, or in Samora, apart from the long horse rides, she dedicated many hours to the pleasures of hunting"[154]. This circumstance was confirmed by the Queen's private letters, "filled with references to wolf, deer, and partridge drives in Samora, Salvaterra, Mafra, Queluz, and Vila Viçosa"[155].

D. Fernando José de Melo established a policy of protection of the environment in the management of royal reserves, characterised by the preservation of the King's hunting space. However, the King was continuously disturbed by an unavoidable calamity of forest fires. These destroyed hunting habitats voraciously, quickly eliminating extensive areas of trees that took years to grow. From 1777 to 1779, during the summer season, fires occurred approximately every two days. From 1779 to 1780, they occurred daily and several times during the day, at the same time in distinct areas[156].

To stop the seasonal summer fire cycle, several measures were taken in 1777. These were continuous inquiries in the game reserves, surprise searches in the houses of reserve inhabitants and officers to find evidence of hunting crimes, and considering inhabitants guilty of "having been the ones who set the fire" whenever fires broke out in their own lands. Protection and watch measures taken by Pina Manique only began to produce results from 1780 onwards. This was with the help of the 1781 Edict, which consecrated capital punishment to armed opposition to reserve guards, as was explained in Chapter 1. From 1782 to 1786, the gap between fires occurrences was of just one week[157].

Sensitive to the difficulties peasants went through in game reserves due to the destruction of their crops by deer and boar, the Surveyor-General appealed to the Queen to grant licences to put nets around the fields, and to cut down the necessary wood to build and repair barns to prevent pigs from destroying crops[158]. Paradoxically, during D. Fernando José de Melo's management, there were almost no grants of licences to farmlands inside reserves, as he makes all efforts to guarantee the preservation of resources and spaces for royal use.

D. Fernando José de Melo died in 1787 and his son, D. Francisco José Luís de Melo, succeeded him, running the Surveyor-General's Department for two years and dying on January 24th 1789, leaving no successor[159]. As in his father's time, the royal family's attention was evident in the care they put in protecting game reserves, and preserving the reserves' resources. The Surveyor-General's Department made a thorough watch over licence grants for felling and clearing lands by fire, making regular inquiries to the game reserves of Ribatejo.

In what concerned the defence of existing resources, D. Francisco José Luís de Melo followed his father's policy and kept the royal prerogatives. As to the recovery of natural resources, he inaugurated a grant of reserve lands for agriculture, using this process as a strategy to renovate the natural heritage with the purpose of recovering and making profitable unused lands destroyed by forest fires or excessive felling.

In February 1789, D. Francisco da Cunha succeeded his cousin in the Surveyor-General's Department[160]. His management corresponded to a mostly turbulent period during which there was a permanent, but ineffective, attempt to maintain royal reserves as they were.

On the one hand, from the seventeen nineties onwards, the royal family visited less regularly both the royal residence of Salvaterra de Magos and the reserves south of the Tagus River. This coincided with the first signs of insanity of Queen D. Maria I. On the other hand, D. João VI loved small game, especially partridge, which was found mainly at the reserves of Lisbon and surroundings, and Sintra[161]. The coercive power the Queen exercised, whether near criminals or near officers, ceased, and in practice, the Surveyor-General was faced with progressive negligence by the reserve guards.

This absence of the royal family from the reserves for large game, as well as the international political situation unfavourable to Portugal (imminent war with Spain) at the turn of the century, and petitions for forest resources to supply the navy's and army's warehouses, necessitated change in reserve resource management policy. The need to supply great quantities of wood to the warehouses of the military bodies, first originated from wood reserves, then from game reserves, made it difficult to preserve dense woods. The alternative was to recover unforested or even unfarmed lands[162]. Óbidos, and above all the Royal Pinewood of Escaroupim, which formed the frontier with the reserves of Coruche and Salvaterra, was the favoured target of the resource renovation policy. This was due to their aptitude for the production of trees and their geographic location, which eased the transportation of timber. As to the lands impoverished by fire, D. Francisco tried to catch the interest of the populations for them to ingeniously, and cleverly, fertilise those lands.

Like his cousin, D. Francisco granted, as a reserve's benefit, the leasehold of plots to the farmers who demanded permission to farm places that were not harmful for game species, "as they do not cause any harm to the reserve"[163]. He did this more frequently than the previous administration.

In the seventeen nineties, the Surveyor-General kept the policy of granting reserve lands for agriculture as a strategy for preserving the royal woods. The incapacity to control the abuse of forest resources with the use of laws and policing force, called for alternative solutions. When granting lands for agriculture, D. Francisco was trying to avoid the quick felling of trees (simultaneously promoting their renovation), to protect the thickets where the game hid, and to restrain forest fires. To do these he authorised agriculture in areas apt for tree planting, and imposed on farmers the condition of planting and treating them. In the areas appropriate for the renovation of thickets, he imposed the condition that these were not to be damaged and that their development should be encouraged. This measure benefited the reserve twice: on one hand, it allowed the recovery of the property; on the other hand, it eliminated potential firebreaks since the protection was made by the same petitioners who were committed to defending the arable land.

Regardless of the impoverishment of lands, licence grants to farm the grounds depend on the acceptance, from tenants and tenants in fee, of the conditions previously imposed. This was recorded in the opinion of the Surveyor-General sent to the King in 1791, "as these thickets are nowadays intersected, due to the many fires that broke there, the petitioner commits to preserve them as long as they are useful for His Majesty's royal amusement: it seems to me that land cultivation would be fruitful, thus ploughing it and making it more prepared through plantations"[164]. This way, as noted in Chapter 1, in 1796 the Surveyor-General tried to stop the hitherto unstoppable agricultural pressure on reserves.

D. Francisco da Cunha changed his policy as soon as the Regulations of 1800 were proclaimed. The reserved area was reduced and the policing system altered. Within the perimeter of royal reserves, the Surveyor-General opposed tendencies towards farmland, since reserves were destined for the preservation of forest and game resources, and not for agricultural development. This position is analysed further when we speak about the internal debate in the Surveyor-General's Department between the Surveyor-General and the general judge of reserves, and consider the position of the minister D. Rodrigo de Sousa Coutinho.

In 1794, however, D. Francisco da Cunha interrupted the management of the Department as he was absent on military campaigns. D. Luís Pinto de Sousa replaced him as the head of the Department. During this period, the authority of the Surveyor-General's Department weakens. The patrols do not fulfil their duties and royal game thieves perform the boldest actions, like breaking down prisons and setting hunting criminals free[165].

D. Francisco came back from his military campaigns in July 1795, but as Governor of Arms of Alentejo and the Algarve, and now living in Tavira, combining that function with the one of Surveyor-General. Being physically apart, the management of royal reserves became less effective. In 1796, to make up for this difficulty, D. Francisco asked for a private post service, so that he could dispatch all matters regarding the Surveyor-General's Department from Tavira. In the following year the post service was granted to him.

Having fully resumed his post as Surveyor-General, he was convinced that it was the large size of the game reserves, as well as the lack of staff of the Department to watch over them, that prevented their preservation as "virgin" spaces. He then suggested to the King the measures that became part of the Regulations of 1800.

However, four years passed between the presentation of his suggestions and the proclamation of the Regulations. During those four years, the Surveyor-General was at the head of royal reserves with the same means, developing activity to keep order and fight back crime.

Between 1798 and 1799, D. Francisco refused several petitions, of peasants and inhabitants of the reserves of Benavente, Salvaterra de Magos and Coruche, to cut down wood and firewood. In November 1799, he advised the Prince Regent to limit all woodcuts at Escaroupim, given the precarious conditions of this pinewood[166]. Private individuals who cut down the trees of the mentioned pinewood made his actions difficult. It was feared that "such an important and interesting piece of land, both for the State and the royal service, be reduced to an unfruitful piece of land with no value whatsoever because of the abuses, the mutilation, and the continuous cuts made for the benefit of private people and for free"[167].

Alongside with the cuts "for free", the persistence of charcoal production sites inside reserves caused concern. The product was destined to provide the capital city with charcoal, and with wood sent to the armies and warehouses in wartime, placed a great pressure on the resource. However, the wood was also threatened by fires carelessly set when preparing fields by burning, and this contributed to their rapid destruction. Moreover, the small-scale reforestation was not enough and too slow to make up for the needs of wood and the renovation of areas for game.

Whilst until the reduction of reserved areas the Surveyor-General had granted land to farm and even encouraged the suppression of parts of the reserves for conversion to agriculture, when the wooded areas were reduced D. Francisco changed his position. He was now mainly bound to preserve the reserved areas so that these could fulfil their functions. The lands needed for sowing had already stopped being reserved. One had to take care of the forest's preservation. Granting reserved lands for agriculture now seemed an enormous danger and the probable cause of destruction of what was left of the Crown's woods. However, he opened some exceptions for unproductive lands that could be renewed through reforestation.

On the other hand, given the first step in the diploma of 1800 for the extinction of part of the Crown's game reserves in a context of agricultural improvement, the way was open to justify the suppression of the remaining unproductive areas of wood reserves. At the turn of the century, D. Francisco faced the dilemma of simultaneously promoting agricultural development, following the dominating "improvement spirit", and protecting reserves from the "improvement argument" by systematically fighting back the pressure to convert them into agricultural land. This issue had been raised previously by noble members of the Academy, namely Domingos Vandelli, in the project of Agrarian Law elaborated in 1788, where he clearly argued that "It would be convenient, for the agricultural argument, that some reserves stopped being reserved areas and several leases were made out of them"[168].

In the same year, the issue of agricultural recovery was raised again, and after the reduction of reserved areas, the controversy is debated and opinions divided. Until the end of D. Francisco's administration, the debate was inflamed between those who supported the preservation of reserves and those who defended their conversion into agriculturally productive spaces. This is seen in the diverse opinions of the reserves' general judge, the Surveyor-General, and D. Rodrigo de Sousa Coutinho[169].

In 1801, the reserves' general judge Manuel Vicente Marcos[170] defended the thesis that wood reserves had everything in their favour with the grant of leases for their unproductive lands. The Surveyor-General's Department was incapable of avoiding the impoverishment of the land and the indiscriminate cut down of "the royal twigs. (...). The aforesaid General Judge referred in his documents to experience having shown that the preservation of those reserved woods in the old way was of no use whatsoever for the Royal Treasury, since the best twigs are cut down and sent away under the false pretext of pruning"[171]. Continuing with his arguments, he agreed with the peasants' complaints and confirmed "the damage caused by that preservation has to be well observed for a solution to be found". Moreover, the means at the disposal of the Surveyor-General's Department proved ineffective in the protection and preservation of woods' resources. At the same time, the imposition of fencing all small farmed areas strongly conditions the lives of peasants: "because the farmers who live close to one another cannot promote the rearing of their cattle (...) and their herds, since many wolves live in those woods and devour their cattle, preventing them from using the land as pastures"[172]. In view of this scenario, the reserves' general judge states that wood reserves would benefit from the conversion of unproductive treeless lands into farmland. It "would be of greater use if the lands in those woods were leased (...), since many of them are appropriate for agriculture"[173]. However, granting land for agricultural exploitation required a clause in favour of the Crown, "reserving nevertheless the twigs that in each of them were found to be worthy of care and preservation, as well as planting and sowing others in the lands improper for any other culture".

If in the period prior to the reduction of game reserves, D. Francisco had promoted its recovery, he endorsed the granting of leases for the impoverished lands of the reserves of Almeirim, Santarém and Óbidos. The Prince also advised his brother, the King, D. João V, to produce special legislation in order to convert the preserve of Almeirim into an appropriate area for growing cereal. However, after the period under which D. Francisco paid enormous interest to the balance between cereal supply and hunting in the area of the Tagus preserves, and throughout the kingdom of D. José I and D. Maria I, the Surveyor-General of the Queen, stopped defending any kind of alienation of land or of the goods in the royal reserves. Due to a gradual impoverishment of the forested and shrub areas fit for game breeding, D. Francisco da Cunha pronounced strongly against the opinion of the general judge of reserves, Manuel Vicente Marcos, "having to move away from the opinion in favour of leases, rejecting such decision, I must, on the contrary, show His Royal Highness that, if put in practise, it will put an end to the royal woods, and consequently to the production of timber so necessary for the Royal

Warehouses"[174]. This statement was based on the bad results private owners presented in the exploitation of natural resources, "making it necessary to present no other proof than the one showing there was no increase whatsoever (...) before the known destruction occurred in the woods of private owners due to their constant inaction"[175]. Fully convinced that granting the exploitation of reserves would lead to full annihilation of forest resources, he concluded, "it is thus beyond any doubt that putting the Royal Woods of Óbidos in the hands of private owners for them to develop the land is in fact contributing to their full destruction"[176]. Besides, the decision of replacing a forested-land by a farmland meant eliminating the new forest growth, "as the land is reduced to an annual culture, all sprouts of which the shoots are usually separated to replace the trees that were cut down are thus extinguished"[177]. On the other hand, the Crown also had nothing to profit from the leases of the woods of Óbidos, since these would go to the hands of "private owners of the State House of Queens, whom the land belongs to"[178].

D. Francisco managed to get his arguments to prevail, and no lease was granted for those lands. Nevertheless, the issue of the conversion of lands of the woods of Óbidos into arable areas would only be resolved in 1801. In the following year, the maintenance of the inalienability of royal reserves was once again questioned. On September 28th 1802, the Surveyor-General was called by the Prince Regent to give his opinion on an Óbidos farmer's petition to lease a parcel of that reserve's woods. On a letter from August 28th, D. João, the Prince Regent, asked for D. Francisco's opinion, reminding him that, regardless of the solution found, the Surveyor-General could not under any circumstance, alienate the reserve's heritage. D. João told him "to bear in mind that the woods were no object to be alienated, and that I should make up for any damage in any other form I would find convenient"[179].

With legal support, and the Prince Regent's confidence, the Surveyor-General confirmed to the sovereign his convictions regarding the bad results of granting leases in royal reserves, and continued his campaign to maintain the "natural order" in reserves. "My opinion regarding the lease and alienation of royal woods is as austere as the one I had the honour to present Your Royal Highness on March 17th of the year 1801. Rejecting the opinion of the general judge of reserves, Manuel Vicente Marcos, I believe that letting the Royal Woods by lease means putting an end not only to the preservation of the few woods existing, but also to the production of the one so necessary"[180]. D. Francisco appealed directly to Prince D. João, asking him to act against the abuse of high nobles and keepers, "I was told that several leases have been credited through the State House of Queens' Council, with the argument that the land of Óbidos is their possession, but all this was made in default of my presence, disregarding regulations which state that the landmarks in any land in those reserves are of no value if I have not seen them myself"[181]. This way D. Francisco sent back to the Crown the issue of the confrontation between the Surveyor-General's Department and the State House of Queens. With the pretext of safeguarding reserve resources, he warned D. João of the fact that the State House of Queens' Council explicitly impinged on royal authority when granting reserved lands, and didn't respect the prerogatives of their magistrates.

In November of that year, the question on the legitimacy of cultivating royal reserve land was once again the issue of the correspondence exchanged between the Prince Regent and D. Francisco José da Cunha. The Count of Caparica made a petition to D. João asking him to release the Delgada Woods, inside the reserve of Óbidos[182]. The Surveyor-General issued an opinion opposing to any kind of alienation of the reserves' heritage. Considering the utmost need for timber to supply the country's warehouses and the navy shipyards, he cautiously suggested the Prince consult the opinion of the War and Navy Ministers before the Regent made a definite decision about releasing the Delgada Woods. These had been marked as a woodland reserve around three hundred years before, and were kept as such, due to Portugal's monarchs' orders to fulfil the need for timber supply to the royal warehouses, and those of the princes and queens, as well as for the war navy[183]. Once again, the Surveyor-General expressed his disagreement with the granting of land for lease. This was an opinion which the Prince Regent appeared to respect, as no document was issued informing the Surveyor-General's Department of any licence granting a lease to private owners inside reserves until the end of 1802.

Nevertheless, several voices rose in favour of the reduction of reserves' unproductive lands being converted into farming areas free from the preserve regime. D. Rodrigo de Sousa Coutinho welcomed the measures taken by the Prince Regent in favour of agriculture in his programme speech, about the development of economy through investment in agrarian activities[184], combining agriculture and forestation. He indeed praised D. João's "initiative" of 1799, as one example of enlightened progress, for the Prince had ordered the reforestation of the royal woodlands of "Pinheiro" with pine and cork trees. The Prince was following the previous recommendation of the General Surveyor of the preserves, to forest unproductive lands inside the royal woodlands. This was presented by D. Francisco José de Melo in the letter of August 8th 1796.

Using the example of the royal initiative and "under the same principles", Sousa Coutinho explored the idea of turning unfarmed lands into productive ones "to encourage more and more the good farming of the lands" and simultaneously obtain sources of raw materials to supply "Lisbon with cheaper fuel and the Royal Navy with abundance of tar and pitch". According to D. Rodrigo, the conversion of forestland into farmland, both out of the waste and unfarmed lands inside reserves, became one of the feasible means to achieve that goal. This was confirmed by the results in sown fields at the reserve of Pinheiro, which "in few years it will stop being an unfarmed land, horrendous to the sight, to become a productive one", where wood and farm products can be found. An effort was made "to grow potatoes in some places of that reserve, promising a great production of this seed, of which an abundant and pleasant food will result"[185].

Regardless of being bound to deal with the position in favour of agriculture, the Surveyor-General made a decision to preserve the existing resources. He also tried to promote a joint action by the Crown and private owners for the defence of pinewoods and woods in general, proposing that Prince D. João should force owners to defend, and watch over their own pinewoods:

"In the reserves of Santarém and Almeirim, until now guarded by thirty-seven officers, there is no wood that does not belong to a private owner. The number of these woods has been reducing, given the little care provided to their owners with regard to the increase and conservation of the woods. It is therefore of great need that, after the improvement measures further indicated are adopted, they be guarded with the same diligence as their owners should show, as these haven forgotten the interests originating from the increases and preservation of those lands"[186].

Side by side with this attempt to preserve the *limes* of the reserve, the Surveyor-General tried to recover the reserved "useless" areas. On April 20th 1805, he informed the Prince of his opinion of a petition to transform unfarmed land into pinewood based on the benefits the production of thickets and twigs would bring as a shelter for game species. In spite of this argument D. João gave a favourable answer, stressing that this licence would only be in force if a lease contract was celebrated, and never a fee-farm contract, thus guaranteeing full ownership of the royal woods[187].

In spite of the Surveyor-General's efforts in the management of royal reserves to keep his functions as General- Surveyor of the royal forests, in his post of command in Tavira in the Algarve, he was quite distant from those areas. However, he could not fulfil both tasks. On one hand, he had military demands to answer to as General Governor of Arms of Alentejo and the Algarve; on the other hand, he was too distant from Lisbon to attend to the royal preserves' demands. Therefore, D. Francisco transferred the management of the Surveyor-General's Department to his son D. Pedro who lived in Lisbon. On February 3rd 1806 D. Pedro sent a communication from the Department informing the wood keeper of Salvaterra and Benavente that, due to "my father's impediment" and "in my administration", he would be the one giving the necessary orders for the Surveyor-General's Department to go on working[188].

D. Pedro da Cunha held the post of Surveyor-General until 1821 and resumed it in 1824 amounting to seven distinct periods. These were 1806 to 1807 until the French invasions (1808-1812); between 1807 and 1808, during Junot's administration; from 1808 to 1812, during the period of the recovery of the Surveyor-General's Department and the expulsion of the French; and from 1812 to 1815, until the signature of the Vienna Treaty. In this interval, the period of compulsory conscription of men in the army and the militia in Portugal ended. Consequently, the officers of the Surveyor-General's Department returned to their posts in the royal reserves. He held it from 1815 to 1820, while national and international political peace were being established. During Beresford's administration, with the Assembly between 1821 and 1823, the counter-revolution and D. João VI's return to the throne in 1824, there was a gap.

Receiving the Surveyor-General's Department from his father's hands in 1806, D. Pedro had to deal with the same management problems of game and wood reserves regarding the preservation and recovery of natural resources. In game reserves, he tried to guarantee abundant game; in wood reserves, he tried to protect the trees necessary for the navy and royal houses; he tried to protect from both natural calamities and from criminals. In wood reserves, this task was even more difficult, as the reserved property "inherited" by D. Pedro contained several areas impoverished by fires. On the other hand, petitions to farm reserved lands persisted. From the beginning of the 19th century onwards, requests to use wastelands inside reserves to transform them into pasture areas intensified. This pressure was greater after the end of the French invasions.

In the year 1806, the Surveyor-General developed an intensive programme to fight the granting of licences to fell royal pinewoods. He blamed the judge of the reserve of Samora for having let firewood be felled without a licence from the Surveyor-General; he questions the judge of the reserve of Santarém on the fulfilment of his and his officers' duties when fires broke in Muja and Salvaterra[189]. The pinewood of Escaroupim was once again at the centre of the Surveyor-General's concerns. On October 23rd 1806, he sent the Prince Regent D. João information on the state of that pinewood. D. Pedro da Cunha asked D. João to stop granting licences to fell trees in that estate, licences which D. João granted without informing the Surveyor-General's Department. The Surveyor-General tried to make the Prince aware of the "reduction" of the pinewood, as well as its difficulty in supplying wood, even for the daily and home use of the Crown. From 1795 onwards, the pinewood had been "eroded", as "many people coveted the pinewood's firewood". Continuous and "abusive cut downs were made during the night, when the guards' vigilance could not be so accurate"[190].

On the other hand, as had happened at the end of the seventeen eighties, in 1807 the movement to clear the woods for agriculture, and requests to farm reserved ground were once again rising in Óbidos, in the Albergaria wood. In 1784, one of the plots of this wood was leased to a tenant in fee for farming. In 1791, another plot of the same wood was leased to Monsignor Rangel, and in 1804 another one to the Countess of Caparica. On July 13th 1807, José Inácio da Costa presented a petition to lease a piece of ground basing his petition on previous precedents[191].

The Surveyor-General carefully analysed the steps necessary to preserve resources, to avoid being deceived by petitioners, but the invasion of reserves was constant, and the response of the watch body to his orders was indifferent or explicitly disobedient. Adding to this state of indiscipline, the Royal Court ran away to Brazil, and the Surveyor-General's Department was put under the direction of the Council of Governors appointed by Prince D. João[192].

Meanwhile, in November the French troops reach Lisbon[193]. Once in power, Junot introduces changes to the head of the Surveyor-General's Department and the management of its resources, as was seen in Chapter 1. On December 9th, the Surveyor-General answered the order issued on the 5th, presenting the game and wood reserves inventory where he informs governors of the Department's week capacity to supply wood from the pinewoods of royal reserves.

After ending the formal restitution of the order at the Surveyor-General's Department, Junot showed interest in knowing the stocks of timber available. On April 26th 1808, D. Pedro da Cunha informed the wood keeper of Setúbal that he had been given orders from the Government to make a new inventory of the "forests and woods fully and presently belonging to the present Government, and that previously belonged to the following owners: the Crown, the House of Queens, the Infantado, and the House of Bragança". The document clarified that from then on, preserves with their officers would be "all gathered under my government", "no districts existing where reserves exist". Carrying out this order, the Surveyor-General wrote a survey of woods, following a detailed form that inquired into the extension of the estate in cause, as well as its revenue and capacity to supply wood. This inquiry had to answer the following:

"1st, name of the province; 2nd, name of the surroundings; 3rd, name of the forest or forests and the quality of the wood it produces; 4th, its approximate extension and width, measured by leagues or ells of the country; 5th, its annual revenue, at least approximately, which can be done by dividing the cost of the cut by the possible number of years of break from one cut to the other; 6th, value of the capital, also approximate; 7th, annual expense with guards and management; 8th, number of guards each wood has; 9th, observations, if existing, naming those woods appropriate to supply the navy and construction"[194].

Curiously, in the same document, D. Pedro informed the purveyor of the circuit court of Setúbal that he did not have to be so strict in the examination: "I believe it needless to observe, given Your Excellency's intelligence, that no accurate or geometric accounts are demanded, as these would demand, instead of six days, six weeks". He probably justified the inaccuracy of the data with the demand of the deadline presented in superior orders, thus enabling him to distort the real information on the possibility of supply of the aforementioned estates.

An exact copy of this letter was sent to the purveyors of Évora, Algarve, Beja, Ourique, Portalegre, Coimbra, Aveiro, Viseu, Lamego, Pinhel, Elvas, Castelo Branco, Santarém, Viana do Castelo, Moncorvo, Porto, Miranda, Penafiel, Braga, Elvas, and Guarda, as well as to the royal magistrates of Vila Viçosa, Aviz, Tomar, Torres Vedras[195]. The magistrates answered the inquiry, mainly from April 30th to May 9th, from the purveyor's offices of Beja, Elvas, Setúbal, Castelo Branco, Lamego, Santarém, Algarve, Tomar, Aveiro, Torres Vedras, Viana, Moncorvo, Miranda, Évora and Viseu. This was along with their counterparts of the circuit courts of Leiria, Mértola, Aviz, Vila Viçosa, Portalegre, Braga, Penafiel, and the magistrates of the districts of Sintra, Samora, Coimbra, Guimarães, Pinhel, and The Treasury of Samora[196].

If, on the one hand, the administrative structure of the Surveyor-General's Department tried to answer the Surveyor-General's requests and the orders of the French government, the lack of means and people, on the other hand, prevented any good results from the controls. Before the French presence, forest fires, illegal charcoal production places, unauthorised felling of thickets and wood, and the transformation of woods into pastures by fire setting were frequent. However, with the French invasions, the destruction of reserves increased enormously[197].

After Junot's expulsion, there was a lack of authority; disrespect towards royal keepers, the army was also in a state of alert permanently pressuring all bodies of the society for military recruitment. A cavalry regiment, that since 1775 helped to patrol the reserves of Santarém and Almeirim during the summer of 1808, ceased to accomplish that task. This decrease in surveillance forces reduced the capacity to defend reserves from fires during the summer season. Answering insistent requests for help from D. Pedro da Cunha, the head of the army, D. Miguel Pereira Forjaz, informed the Surveyor-General of the royal forests on October 4th 1808 that, as soon as possible, he would send a detachment to the King's forests. Nevertheless, it was impossible for him to honour the promise, as he had no troops to spare.

During the French invasions and the presence of the British army, defenceless royal reserves were at the mercy of both the subjects of His Royal Portuguese Highness[198] and the army of His British Majesty[199]. Furthermore, the population had been armed to fight the enemy. The Surveyor-General warned the captain of the Ordinances of Samora to arm "your people as had been determined", recommending, "that you do it in such a way that the use of guns only has the purpose of defending the State and never the one of putting an end to game"[200]. Until the disarmament of the population was completed and the authority of the Surveyor-General's Department over its officers and local communities was fully restored, the situation remained difficult. Some time elapsed after Junot's expulsion and the "return" of the Surveyor-General's post to the hands of D. Pedro José de Melo e Cunha; the latter returning as Surveyor-General in 1809[201].

D. Pedro was shown to be an intelligent manager, but without the resources to put his ideas into practice. He had no officers, as many were in the army and others refused to fight. Besides, by now the population was armed and the number of criminals was superior to the number of guards. In such conditions, fighting crime was very difficult, and this was in spite of numerous edicts and threats against "malefactors", "scoundrels", "evil-doers", "villains", "murderers", that is to say, reserve criminals.

His care with reserves and the will to impose his authority as Surveyor-General, even against his peers, led him to ignore direct orders from D. João VI. In 1810 and 1811, the King had instructed him twice to grant a licence for felling for the Duke of Cadaval to cut down his pine trees in Muge. On the contrary, for the second time D. Pedro failed to obey D. João's orders. The Duke of Cadaval informed the monarch and in 1812, D. João warned the Surveyor-General not to disobey him again; a warning which D. Pedro finally obeyed[202].

Very slowly, D. Pedro managed to restore some order in the administration of woods and the exploitation of arable land, while trying to avoid leasing the few woods still left. He tried to make the areas transformed by fire or by the clear-felling of trees profitable as farming or forest areas.

On the other hand, the Surveyor-General encouraged the cutting down of thickets and granted more licences to clear scrub areas. His suggestion is that an end be put to all restrictions on the use of woods. In these areas, previous prohibitions to their use, now became an urgent need. It was even desirable that farmers cut down branches, clean the woods and use trees for their own interest. What was carefully bought and sold to farmers was now given, as a way to encourage woods' cleaning to prevent forest fires. From 1810 onwards, the difficulty in finding skilled workmen to cut down woods in royal reserves was enormous. In the reserve of Pancas, the possibility of keeping the effective prohibition on the cutting of wood and, in compensation, granting populations licences to cut and clean woods, was considered. At the same time, D. Pedro continued promoting reforestation favoured by the granting of plots for agriculture.

From 1808 onwards, the Surveyor-General granted farmers licences to take their cattle to pasture on unfarmed lands of the reserves, with a greater frequency than it had ever been done by the Surveyor-General's Department. In global terms, licences requested and granted to exploit soils were fewer than in the period before the French invasions. What came out more frequently were petitions to use wasteland (mainly from Alcácer, Pinheiro, Pera e Comporta, and Santarém). This situation was maintained until the Constitutional Assembly and encouraged by the proclamation of the decree of the 15th of April 1815 (noted earlier). The general wood keeper of Samora invoked that decree, in what concerned the "public usefulness" of the transformation of wastelands into farmlands, to obtain the licence necessary for the inhabitants of the village of Samora to farm a wasteland that was used as a common pasture area.

It is true that the reserve of Almeirim had been abolished and the land belonging to it had been destined for agriculture by the diploma of March 21st 1800. The reserve's extension, that included the area from Ribeira de Muge up to the Surroundings of Abrantes, constituted an area of relevant dimensions. Perhaps the offer of land for agriculture resulted in less tension between agriculture and reserves. The record of information on conflicts having decreased from 1812 to 1815, the greater control on reserve resources was now felt through the granting of wasteland conversion. Until the invasions, inhabitants and farmers requested wastelands for communal use, these tended now to be leased to a single individual who entered into conflict with the wider community. As with the rest of the country, following the same movement to take over the commons, some tried their luck to carry it out in the royal preserves[203].

During the years from 1816 to 1820, the reserve management started to return to normality. The confirmation of validity for plots' lease contracts was resumed; peasants recovered the habit of operating within the law, making the necessary petitions to obtain licences to cut down wood and trees for domestic use[204]; wolf hunts were resumed[205], as well as the control of licences to use reserved pastures[206]. Policing now recovered and the Surveyor-General was acknowledged as supreme head of the Department. The annual cycle of threatening speech in the summer season, linked to the frequency of forest fires, was once again recurring in the letters sent by the Surveyor-General both to game and to wood reserve judges.

Reforestation, in turn, seemed to proceed well in Salvaterra. D. Pedro paid compliments to the patrol corporal of this reserve for the success of the pine nut sowing, reminding him, nevertheless, of the need to clean pinewoods to avoid fires spreading[207]. On the other hand, the pinewood of Escaroupim still suffered all kinds of thefts. In spite of these difficulties, the Surveyor-General tried to control the situation by opening inquiries into royal reserves in December of 1818. However, an incapacity to eliminate crime occurrences persists, especially in game reserves, as is still shown in the correspondence of 1820.

In 1821, after the extinction of open game reserves and the Surveyor-General having lost his power over royal parks, he limited himself to managing the Crown's wood reserves. This included supervising wood felling and the reforestation of the wood reserves of Óbidos, Escaroupim, and Pinheiro until August of 1821[208]. In 1824, as discussed in Chapter 1, D. João VI fully restored the diploma of 1800, giving back to the Surveyor-General the management of game reserves, but withdrawing from him the power to manage wood reserves. Thus, D. João changed the actors, but kept the measures taken by the Constitutional Assembly regarding the separation of entities managing the Crown's woods. For these, he created a forest management project that revealed his knowledge as a forest expert, and his intention to make them profitable through their production, and not only by restraining the use of their resources[209].

2.3.2. Game resources

The management of game resources consisted mainly of taking strict measures to defend royal game species. It consisted of never granting licences to hunt deer, fallow deer and boar; and of carefully controlling licences given to hunt small game like the rabbit, the hare, partridges and ducks which were attributed to the Surveyor-General's Department officers, judges and reserve inhabitants, peasants or individuals with any kind of practical occupation. The strict control on licensed hunting was accompanied by stricter reprisals with strong punishments - with prison, whipping, galleys, and, in the case of nobles, with exile, for whoever dared hunt the King's game species in royal reserves.

Royal game reserves existed to satisfy "royal pleasure". Managing game reserves meant guaranteeing the supply of enough species for the King to hunt whenever he wished.

Besides this mission, the Surveyor-General's Department managed across the whole country the hunting of the most feared wild animal of rural communities: the wolf. In royal reserves, wolf hunts were one of the Department's obligations. However, under this pretext, the Surveyor-General had the power to appoint the gamekeepers able to hunt wolves in the country's municipalities, thus troubling municipal powers in all municipalities of the kingdom. The duty of protecting rural communities allowed the Surveyor-General's Department to extend its influence to the whole country.

Inside game reserves, part of the lands were farmed and arable crops were often damaged, both by large and small game. Restrictions in favour of the exercise of hunting, imposed on reserve inhabitants and consecrated in legislation proclaimed between 1777 and 1782, made living conditions of those communities much harder.

In those years, the legislation forbidding the use of guns and licences to use firearms in reserves, granted to any individuals who did not belong to the body of guards, was resumed. According to the Judge of Santarém, this legislation had become obsolete some 150 years ago. The law was in force but no one operated within it. In 1779, with no other options but to survive through crime, the peasants appealed to the Queen, asking her to allow them to fence their sown fields with fishing nets to protect them from deer, as her father, King D. José, had allowed the inhabitants of Pera e Comporta in 1754. Sensitive to the arguments of reserve inhabitants, who were powerless to fight back in this tragedy, since hunting was a crime severely punished, the Surveyor-General granted this request[210].

The use of nets arose as the only means authorised by Queen D. Maria I for farmers to be able to defend themselves from animals living in forests. This grant is a single grace, granted case by case, i.e. only for game reserve inhabitants who applied officially and was precarious: if deer were wounded in the nets the grace would stop immediately and the crops would be defenceless. The same would also happen if the nets were used not as a defence tool but as hunting traps. The request to use nets was awarded in 1791 and renewed in 1795, to the inhabitants of Salvaterra and Benavente[211].

At the reserve of Samora and at the estates of Abiul and Monte Novo, farmers tried another alternative by the Surveyor-General and the King: protecting themselves from game by firing dry gunpowder shots[212]. D. Maria granted this licence, which was later revealed as a way of prevarication, since, under the cover of permission to carry a gun, the inhabitants used real bullets to hunt wild game and the royal mallards of the fen of Comporta[213]. But the justification was not arbitrary, because, whenever the Surveyor-General heard rumours about it, he did not have licences to use dry gunpowder cancelled without previously checking whether there was a crime. Only when a crime was verified did he cancel those licences including to carry guns. He then documented the accusations and started criminal proceedings.

Besides protecting sown fields, the Surveyor-General's Department tried to keep a strict control on hunting licences to guarantee the preservation of reserves. Those were given solely and exclusively for small game: rabbits, hares, sparrows, ducks and partridges. As can be proved by the lists of hunting licences from the Surveyor-General's Department, over twenty-three years, from 1777 to 1800, this rule was fulfilled with the utmost strictness[214]. During this period, the Surveyor-General only granted and inscribed in the lists of the institution hunting licences for partridges and hares in the reserves of Ribatejo. These were more frequent in the reserve of Lisbon and the surrounding areas.

Therefore, with the help of the protection measures for arable lands and controlled licences granted for small game to the inhabitants of reserves, the Surveyor-General's Department adopted a formula of commitment, which allowed it to peacefully safeguard game resources. Yet, as seen in Chapter 3, the day-to-day operation of game reserves was ruled by violence and evasion to established rules. Poaching was the prevailing rule.

Besides, in large game reserves, according to the official records available, a lord could not even hunt, unless he had a spoken licence and was in the company of the King, during hunting expeditions in Salvaterra and, for some years, in Vila Viçosa. For 44 years, from 1777 to 1821, comparing the lists where licences are registered[215] with the Correspondence Copy Book[216], only three licences for large game were found. These were granted to title-holders of the kingdom, allowing them to shoot deer and fallow deer. Two were granted to the Count of Óbidos, uncle of the Surveyor-General, for his estate and entailed estate of Pancas, of which he was the owner. In the reserves of Ribatejo only one licence was granted, this was so that

Gamekeepers could send the Surveyor-General D. Francisco some deer and boar pieces for the wedding of his son D. Pedro. However, in some cases, Queen D. Maria and King D. João granted spoken licences to title-holders of the kingdom without notification to the Surveyor-General's Department. These licences however, were not part of the official record of the Department. Those were registered in letters sent by the Surveyor-General to the title-holders themselves, asking for certificates or a confirmation of the licences granted by Their Majesties, as seen in the letter of the Duke of Cadaval on December 2nd 1782 to an aristocrat of the court:

"Having certified myself that Your Excellency has been hunting and also has dogs sent to hunting expeditions, with your weapons, to hunt all kind of game in the royal reserve of Sintra, I assumed Your Excellency was in possession of a royal determination: this one however not existing, I have created one, as I am obliged to by my post. I hope to have the King's favour and find His Majesty's resolution to inform me of this, so I can put in writing what His Highness decided. This is why I would like Your Excellency to inform me of the order you had on this subject, so I can carry out my obligations"[217].

On the other hand, whenever any diplomatic entity visited Portugal, the Surveyor-General's Department was instructed to hunt deer and boar in reserves for large game, so that sovereigns could give presents to their guests. Later the French government maintained the same attitude. In royal reserves, only people of excellence, such as high-ranking French officers, could hunt. This same policy was later followed during Wellington's government with regard to British officers.

Licences to catch small game, rabbits and hares, were usually allowed annually, from March to November each year[218]. November to March coincided with the period during which the royal family stayed at the reserves of the Tejo[219]. The renewal of licences was frequent and presented no problems. They were granted without distinction of social origins. What socially differentiated the practice of hunting rabbits and hares were the technique and the means used with or without firearms, with or without dogs, and, when allowed to hunt with dogs, with what kind of breed, and whether with or without consent to hunt with packs. Usually, farmers and inhabitants with a craft, shoemaker or other, were awarded the right to hunt rabbits and hares with sticks, sometimes with nets and in some cases with one or two bloodhounds, but never with greyhounds or packs of dogs. Sometimes, but rarely, they were also granted permission to use firearms and a bloodhound to hunt in the reserves of Ribatejo. In the royal fens in Sintra, hunting birds like ducks and quail ("birdies")[220] was a privilege of the officers of the Surveyor-General's Department, i.e. Wood Keepers, Gamekeepers, and Reserve Judges. From 1777 to 1800, hunting licences for one single day were frequent and were granted both to municipality and reserve officers, to hunt birds with the use of firearms and one or two dogs in the fens of Muge, Pera e Comporta, and Sintra. These licences were granted exclusively to "honourable people", for one day only, so that they "would not get used to abusing the reserves"[221]. A way of controlling these licences was giving the boatmen from Santarém an order to "only consent to transporting" men with a rifle "to the banks of royal reserves", these being "bearers of one-day licences", so "they can amuse themselves hunting quails during the summer time".

Licences granted to the senior people of the country always included permission to use firearms and dogs to hunt hares, rabbits and sometimes partridges. However, the use of greyhounds was an exclusive privilege of royals. Apart from the capture of hares and large animals, partridges were a kind of game much appreciated by royal personages. Licences to hunt them were a privilege usually linked to nobility, being especially attributed for Sintra and Lisbon. The licences included permission to use firearms, which was an exception. From D. João VI's regency onwards, there was increased protection for partridges, as well as growing restrictions on licences allowing their hunting.

Prince D. João reserved himself the exclusive right to capture and hunt partridges in all royal reserves, which resulted in the Surveyor-General's obligation to send to Rio de Janeiro 68 partridges destined for D. João's amusement or for the royal table. During the French invasions, from 1809 to 1812, the order of partridges to satisfy his majesty's appetite was no doubt the main worry of the Surveyor-General's Department. This was indeed the King's sole demand, as he showed to be either fully unacquainted with the country's reality or very indifferent to the Department's situation.

In short, the social differentiation of licences was made in two ways: large game hunting was an exclusive right of the King. Hares and rabbits could be hunted by all, but these occurred in distinct periods of time and, above all, by different means, like firearms and dogs. Ducks living in well-defined waterways were a "prize" for the resident officers of royal reserves, and associated with their post.

If game species' hunting was strictly controlled, wolf hunting followed a different logic. Killing, destroying and, if possible, exterminating this species was the priority. Of all harmful animals, the canine predator was considered the worst destroyer, as it killed flocks, herds, and reputably, people. Foxes and weasels also entered this list of animals to kill, but the wolf was the preferential target of peasants and farmers' complaints, as well as of the attention of the Surveyor-General and even the King. Since 1777, the order to make wolf hunts from January to May was constant, but increasing in the spring and summer. If until the French invasions populations gathered to take part, voluntarily or compulsorily, in the hunts of the peasant's' most feared adversary, after the invasions the situation changed. Yet, it changed in a curious way. Military mobilisation resulted in the abandonment of fields and peasants complained more and more against the lack of wolf hunts. On the other hand, whenever the Surveyor-General organised them, farmers did not attend. Curiously enough, perhaps because he needed to impose his authority or to calm down populations and solve economic problems, one of the Surveyor-General's first measures after the French left was in giving orders for wolves to be hunted in royal reserves. This was especially in Salvaterra, Benavente, Coruche, Samora, Pinheiro, Pancas, and Alenquer. From 1812 onwards, there was constant demand for wolves to be hunted, both in royal game reserves and in the pinewoods of Azambuja and Alenquer das Senhoras Rainhas. From 1812 to 1820, this ritual was carried out annually in game and wood reserves, as had happened when the royal family went to the reserves in the south.

The appointment of wolf hunters created enormous legal and administrative conflicts, resulting in court processes and numerous exchanges of letters between the Surveyor-General's Department and the municipalities of the kingdom[222]. The *Desembargo do Paço* acted as judge in these conflicts and confirmed that it was the Surveyor-General, and not the municipalities, who was entitled to appoint wolf hunters. It also clarified that wolf hunters, and not territorial judges, were the only ones entitled to carry out this kind of hunt. In addition, the municipalities' officers and magistrates had to provide all the necessary help for wolf hunters to carry out their mission.

If judicially the Surveyor-General's Department was acknowledged for its achievements, in terms of crimes associated with fires and poaching, its effectiveness was limited. This is considered in the next chapter.

3. PRIVILEGES AND CONFLICTS

As explained in previous chapters, the forest was the primary location for hunting and the source of timber for the navy and for domestic use. However, while wood reserves acquired a more and more utilitarian status, game reserves gained a symbolic force as privileged places for the royal family.

From the Middle Ages until the end of the Ancient Regime, hunting was part of the aristocratic *ethos*. Unchanged by political, religious and socio-economic movements, its practice was always claimed as one of the main activities connected to leisure and to the training of the knight and the nobleman. The French Revolution broke up with this idyllic formula established in favour of nobility, and legitimised both hunting and the use of the forest as citizenship rights. Through time and especially in moments of political-ideological disruption, hunting and the right to hunt became targets of dispute among social and political forces. In the context of the emerging liberalism, hunting discourse recovered both the original texts from Classic Antiquity, as well as Medieval and Renaissance elements, justifying, in its origins and in time, the aristocratic praxis of hunting as an element linked to the foundation of monarchy.

After the French Revolution, the exercise of hunting was claimed by citizens as a rightful conquest. This process occurred in Portugal in 1821, in Spain in 1812[223], and in France in 1789, seven days after the takeover of the Bastille: "Le décret du 11 août s'en était tenu à n'autoriser la chasse qu'aux seuls propriétaires et laissait a des lois de police ultérieures la faculté de réglementer son exercice. Les députés de l'Assemblé Nationale, dans leur majorité, consideraient le droit de chasse comme un attribut du droit de propriété"[224]. And if the European nobility of the Ancient Regime had left numerous material testimonies consecrating hunting as an element of distinction, in the monarchic counter-revolutions of France, Spain and Portugal the monarchies of the 1800s, claiming they were the heirs of that prestige, invoked hunting and restrictions to its practice as a privilege of kings and aristocracy. In the 19th century, also in reference to hunting, the dispute between the "Ancient Regime order" and the "Liberal order" was played out by monarchic restoration movements and constitutional liberal movements.

3.1. Aristocratic ethos and hunting

During the Middle Ages, great hunting treatises like the ones by Gaston Phoebus, D. João de Portugal and Alfonso XI of Castile were written. Throughout the Modern Age several original treatises on hunting were produced, like the works of Nuñez Avenduño and Alonso Martínez de Espinar, written in the 16th century, or the treaty of Pero Menino and the reflections of Manuel Severim de Faria, dating from the 17th century[225]. Following the Renaissance, these works recovered elements from mythology, philosophy, and politics of Classic Antiquity. Apart from this, these new texts included recently acquired knowledge from the New World, being influenced by these discoveries, as can be seen in the work of Argote de Molina that described hunting in Europe, Africa, India and South America.

On the other hand, during the Modern Ages, the appropriation of woodland resources and of the use of the forest originate a reflection at the level of law, supported by a theological justification that legitimised hunting and fishing as every man's natural right. In 1593, Nuñez de Avenduño stated, "luego que Dios creó los hombres les pertenció este derecho de sujetar las bestias y aves: (…) este derecho de cazar las dichas bestias, y aves, y peces, es tan propio de los hombres, que ningún Emperador, ni Rey, ni outro Príncipe inferior no lo puede quitar, ni vedar a los súbditos, y si lo quita, o veda sin causa, haze fuerza, y violencia, y peca mortalmente"[226]. He justified, however, the full possession of woodland and forest goods moving inside the owner's land limits by basing it on property right, thus justifying the creation of reserves and the hunting activity as an exceptional practice of kings and emperors.

In Portugal, until the end of the Ancient Regime, hunting treatises refer exclusively to large game hunting as performed by the King or by court nobility. They do not refer to ordinary hunting, "a modest exercise of the good bourgeois, the rural disciple of Saint Hubert, in which killing by gunshot is made with less science, in which there is more amusement, and in which much less is spent"[227]. Only from the second half of the 19th century onwards does one find in Portugal hunting manuals on small game species made for the common hunter[228]. On the other hand, critiques considering hunting as a reproachful practice, which had been made periodically by Church Fathers like St. Augustine or by writers like Cervantes through his character Sancho Pança, seemed to have few followers at the level of literature[229].

In Portugal, hunting was sanctioned even by the theological considerations developed by Manuel Severim de Faria, showing that over time the Catholic Church had developed a debate around the legitimacy of hunting as an activity pleasing to God or not. Though St. Augustine had condemned hunting because it drove people away from both praying and politics, Severim de Faria refutes this with other arguments. He presented hunting as an economic, useful, and necessary activity for the survival of humans, morally justified as a guarantee of chastity, and therefore worthy of emperors and kings. He stated, "This exercise serves therefore to preserve chastity, and that is why ancients worshipped Diana, inventor of hunting, as goddess of that virtue, and Seneca introduces Hypolitus as a chaste hunter, and from disdainer of the disorderly affection between Phedra & Horacious his effect passes on to those who get married"[230].

In the 16th and 17th centuries, the reprinting of medieval hunting treatises and judicial-theological debates on this activity seem to be a mark of the importance this practice had for Western European monarchs. Filipe II of Portugal publishes a series of hunting treatises in Portugal and Spain, reprinting in 1616 both Books of the Surveyor-General's Department by D. João de Portugal and Pero Menino[231]. In 1624, he promoted the printing of the *Tratado de Monteria* by Argote de Molina, written in 1582.

In the 18th century, this literary production declined, although some essays were written, such as the one by Beneton de Perrin, who wrote a work in 1734 called *Eloge Historique de la Chasse*[232]. In this he praised the virtues of monarchy and the hunting practices inherent to it. This work was set in the context of protection of hunting and the importance given by several European monarchies to the preservation of royal reserves. It is worth recalling that the Black Act was passed in England in 1722, which set the death penalty for those caught poaching inside royal or aristocratic reserves. In 1733, in Portugal, the edict setting capital punishment for that same crime, if followed by evasion or explicit aggression to reserve guards, was issued. The following year the aforementioned work was published in France, not only giving importance to the virtues of hunting but also presenting a description of all French monarchs who protected and sponsored hunting.

By the end of the Ancient Regime, and in the first quarter of the 19th century, after the French Revolution, it is clear both the reprints of hunting and nobility treatises, produced between the 16th and 18th centuries, and the more recent literary production showed the privileges of that social group, in a context of reaffirmation of monarchies as opposed to the liberal movement.

Beneton de Perrin's work was reprinted in Paris in the year 1824, when Portugal and France observed the recovery of the order of the Ancient Regime's, and Charles X began ruling in France. But whereas in France Charles X did not restore the old privileges associated with the reserves, in Portugal D. João VI reasserted the legislation on royal reserves as it existed before the Revolution[233].

When speaking about the importance of hunting in the foundation of the monarchic system, in the work previously mentioned, Beneton de Perrin recalled an author of Classic Antiquity, Plinius, "La Chasse, selon Pline, a donné naissance aux Etats Monarchiques (…). Dans les premiers temps, les hommes ne possédaient rien en propre ; ils vivaient sans crainte & sans envie : & n'ayant d'autres ennemis que les bêtes sauvages, leur seule occupation était des chasseurs, de sorte que celui qui avait le plus d'adresse & de force se rendait le chef des Chasseurs de sa contrée". In addition, the chief that protects the community by force rules over all others. Perrin developed all his arguments by presenting a close link between hunting and the leaders in France, from the Roman Empire until the reign of Louis XV, in the 18th century.

At the beginning of the 19th century, memoirs by the nobility and judicial literature present hunting as a privilege of aristocracy. These works already show a language justifying the maintenance of the order of the Ancient Regime, probably as a reaction to liberal ideology.

In Portugal, words praising the privileges of the nobility can be found in the treatise by Pereira de Oliveira from 1805, in the reprint of texts by Manuel Severim de Faria from 1806, and in the judicial reflections on agrarian law by Porfírio Hemétrio Homem de Carvalho from 1815. In his work, the bachelor presented hunting as an obligation of every nobleman's education, referring this clause to Pombal's diploma from 1776. Porfírio de Carvalho interpreted Pombal's legislation as applicable to the whole kingdom and stated, "no person can hunt" without a civil nobility degree "that distinguishes the order of citizens from the body of the common people"[234]. In addition, the state of nobility, "civil or political, is a quality granted by the Prince, directly or implicitly, or acquired by prescription in consequence of old possessions"[235]. By creating a reserve for the nobility, natural and civil, the minister D. José was considering hunting as one of the elements for the *aristocratic ethos* to stand out.

In all these works, one finds a common element: the legitimisation of the exercise of hunting as an element linking monarchy, nobility and private property. Private property is no longer subject to the *res nulius* principle, and so the game existing inside it is linked to its owner. Natural law, which allowed all individuals the practice of hunting (according to Nuñez Avenduño), is undervalued, and the predominance of property law grants this right exclusively to the owner. This claims the legitimacy to reserve Crown properties. However, the reserve regime applied to the forest by the Portuguese and Spanish Crowns overcomes and violates property law, since royal reserves interfere with the property rights of private owners because the royal reserves include properties from both municipalities and private owners. The liberal movements of the 19th century used natural and property law as major arguments to claim private property as a right of every citizen, and thus abolish the exclusivity of appropriation of woodland goods.

Apart from a judicial and literary justification, the Modern Ages produced a material legacy at the level of physical occupation, painting, architecture, and tile production, which revealed the importance of hunting in the daily life of aristocracy.

As the humanist movement grew, as religious divisions between Catholics and Protestants became more serious, the need to assert the territorial and ideological *status quo* took an increased production of visible testimonies to convey the new order of thinking. A material language was developed at the level of art that portrayed the interests and life practices of the nobility. Those who ordered and sponsored the construction of palaces and the production of works of art wished to leave their personal mark in the works produced. On the other hand, these have greater importance according to the author that produces them. This way the representation of the hunting activity assumed a special importance inside aristocracy and in the great European Courts.

With regard to painting, following the course of the movements adopted in Western and Southern countries like Portugal and Spain, monarchs had themselves represented alongside their royal hunting dogs – greyhounds. An example of this are the portraits of D. Sebastião which are part of the collection of the Museum of Ancient Art in Lisbon[236], and the paintings of

Philip IV of Spain by Velazquez[237], as well as the portrait of a deer that is included in the collection of the Prado Museum in Madrid[238].

In Saxony, Lucas Cranach, official painter to Frederic the Wise and a personal friend of Luther, represented group scenes of the daily life of the aristocracy, like deer hunts, and not just religious motifs or the individual portrait of the King as represented by the Catholic Western Southern school. These can be seen in the Kunsthistorisches Museum of Vienna.

Christian civilisation associates the iconographic symbol of the deer to God. This animal represents the beginning and the end, the Alpha and the Omega, renovation and the cycle of the eternal returning[239]. This representation of God in the form of a deer was portrayed by Dürer in his Vision of St Eustace, which is included in the assets of the Galleria Doria in Rome, and on the portal of Saint Hubert's chapel in Amboise (see Picture 1 in the iconographic annex) as a manifestation of the Creator to Saint Hubert, patron saint of hunting. The deer is also seen as the symbol of nobility. In the coats of arms' room in the Palace of Sintra, where the coats of arms and weapons of the noble houses of Portugal are depicted, the deer can be seen amid other pictures.

With regard to architecture, the hunting pavilions built by the European royal houses in the 16th and 17th centuries showed the importance of hunting in the daily life of the Court. In France, Francis I ordered a hunting pavilion to be constructed by Leonardo da Vinci, the castle of Chambord[240] (see Picture 2 in the iconographic annex). This structure, due to its monumental aspect, the contrast of colours, (white – black), and the absence of gardens around it, irrupts, at the end of the woods and after an opening in the woods. This is like an immense white body closed from behind by a dense set of trees, suggesting an unequivocal image of power and fear, as can be perceived by the sentence that, according to oral tradition, was said by Francis I when referring to the construction of this mighty building, "Dieu et moi au même étage".

In Portugal, the construction of royal palaces since the Middle Ages inside the game reserves, like the ones in Almeirim and Sintra and afterwards the one of Salvaterra de Magos, was also iconic. These imply through the construction of buildings, the importance of hunting for the dynasties of Avis and Bragança.

Apart from buildings and spaces destined for hunting and hare hunting (on horseback and with greyhounds)[241], falconry[242] (hunting with birds of prey) was a very important activity

82

among the entire European aristocracy, with a clear decline from the second half of the 18th century onwards[243]. Exchanging hawks between the ruling houses of Europe was an important diplomatic practice and a sign of good terms between monarchies. Giving hawks as presents was the most important symbol of peace and the seal of good terms between both parties[244].

The Royal Falconry of Salvaterra de Magos received hawks from Denmark and Malta through the 18th century[245]. If D. João and D. José had granted falconry an important role among royal hunting activities[246], in the reigns of D. Maria and D. João I this activity declines, since these two monarchs preferred hunting and partridge hunting, respectively. The Royal Falconry of Salvaterra de Magos however goes on operating, all its staff and equipment being preserved in full. The Chief Falconer went on working and hawks were fed and treated regularly[247].

The reception of the hawks from Malta and Denmark had to follow a strict protocol. All staff had to be present at the Belém pier wearing a festive uniform. The Chief Falconer had to be at Court and the crew of the brigantine (see picture 3 in the iconographic annex) took the hawk from Lisbon to Salvaterra de Magos. The Queen always granted a personal hearing to the representative of the Holy Religion of Malta who delivered the hawk, receiving him in the morning with a guard of honour. This ritual is performed every year from 1785 until 1796[248]. In spite of showing a special interest in hunting (as shall be seen in Point 3.1.2.), D. Maria I fulfils the whole protocol necessary for a worthy reception representing the symbol of friendship between both monarchies[249].

In Portugal, however, in the 18th century, more than the written texts, tile panels record the importance of hunting in the daily life of aristocracy, reflected in the decoration of palaces. An example of this are the tiles from the Seminary of Santarém (see Pictures 3 to 17 in the iconographic annex), representing the landscape and hunting techniques described in treatises, including the chases in the New World, in Africa, in India, and on the American continent. The scenes depicted in the bishop's palace of Santarém portray a deer hunt with slipknot ropes in the marshy lands of the Tejo, where a large part of the royal reserves existed.

Through the Ancient Regime, the practice of hunting continues in spite of their agents' change or of new ideological concepts. Hunting was legitimised as a product of creation by the Book of Genesis and by the Old Testament in general, as well as an economic activity essential to human survival. With the humanist movement, it fits in the recovery of the arguments of the classics. Moreover, in spite of the religious disputes that took place with the Reformation, the praxis of hunting is unconditionally defended by aristocracy. Liberal revolutions will see it as a citizenship right and monarchic counter-revolutions as a symbol of the recovery of power.

3.2. Royal stays

During the reigns of D. Maria I and D. João VI, attention given to hunting by kings was heavily felt. The royal family's hunting calendar occupied eight to nine months of the year.

In the "Descrição das Coutadas e Casas de Campo dos Príncipes de Portugal"[250] [Description of the Reserves and Country Houses of the Princes of Portugal] one can see the favourite routes taken by D. Maria I and her father D. José during their hunting stays. Through this itinerary, let us gently prepare to take part in the description of the Crown's summer and winter game reserves and follow the map of the reserves of Santarém (Figures 1 and 2).

"The most remarkable and pleasant river of Lisbon, joyful and peaceful in spring and summer time (…); it brings comfort to fishery and the use of the carbine. One and a half miles from Court, in the same sea river, are the places of Alcântara and Belém, healthy and abundant in game like partridges, hares, rabbits, and deer."

"Twelve miles away, on the huge headland Mount Artabo, or moon mountain, to which sailors call Rock and natives call Sintra sierra, a royal and most noble palace is set, famous for its buildings and gardens, and holding the name of the same small town".

Maintaining this register, the anonymous author reported the characteristics of the Arrábida Sierra and the frequency with which the Court went to its reserves, as well as its "country house, set on the most fertile, attractive and healthy villages of Azeitão". He then described the reserve of Pancas: "Nine miles away from Lisbon, on the other side of the river banks, where one can go to by boat, using the comfortable and safe brigantines, making a few-hour way and coming back in the same day, is the famous reserve of Pancas". He then moves the account to the south: "A few miles further, near the Great Town of Setúbal, by the arms of the river Sado, are the two big and famous reserves of Pinheiro and Palma". Following the map, one can see that "away some 30 and 42 miles from the Court are the royal Country Houses of

Salvaterra and Almeirim, linked to the sea by the river Tejo. The road by land is easy, gentle and comfortable"[251].

The reserves of Salvaterra and Almeirim had excellent conditions for the Court to enjoy fully the multiple hunting activities. During the forty-day winter hunting stay, the royal family would be accompanied by the Court, finding great pleasure in the "diverse entertainments and comfortable exercises". Landscape, abundance of game and the easiness with which ladies could watch from the plane, the shows performed by hunters when chasing their prey, were a very important contribution to this delight[252].

"They are abundant in boar, deer, and all species of game. They are comfortable for horse riding, easy for boar hunters and hunters with rifles, abundant in falconry. They are set for the entertainment of the ladies, who can enjoy such comfort and amusement that, from their own carriages, they watch rabbits being killed, deer being caught with ropes, hares and rabbits running and birds flying. All this done so gently and with no fatigue that in the great distance they are careless in their zeal"[253].

Besides this hunting Eden of Salvaterra and Almeirim, the author carried on with his description, mentioning the reserve of Vila Viçosa, ninety miles away from Lisbon, and describing it as "the most famous of the peaceful House of Bragança".

After having mentioned the royal reserves regularly visited by the royal family and the Court, the author referred to the "inspiring" and peace-making role of reserves as places more appropriate for amusement than government, as well as favourable places for the Court to give proof of its devotion to "the cult of Majesty". Reserves were "the most noble of all places for all Princes (...); for the kingdom's expeditions, they are the most important place of the whole Empire, very much appropriate for human entertainment and political government". One can even doubt whether it would be "more appropriate for pleasure than for government".

Nevertheless, the amusements and pleasures of the Court ended in the early seventeen nineties. D. Maria I's illness enforced an interruption to hunting stays from 1792 onwards. Two years later, on November 10th 1794, the fire at the Ajuda Palace forced the royal family to move from Lisbon to Queluz[254]. After the illness of the Queen Mother and the departure from the Ajuda Palace, the hunting stays at Salvaterra ceased, although the ones at Mafra, Queluz,

Sintra, and occasionally Vila Viçosa, carried on. These included the one D. João VI in 1796, offered his father-in-law the King of Spain, to allow his wife D. Carlota to be with her father[255].

By the end of the 18th century, hunting was such an important activity in the life of the royal family that, as one can see in Table 1, the calendar of "royal stays" outside Lisbon was conditioned by the hunting season, only interrupted by the religious calendar.

Table 1
Hunting calendar of the royal family between 1778 and 1800[1]

Year	Day/Month	Description
1778	**17th January to 7th March**	**Stay at Salvaterra**
	17th January	Departure to Salvaterra
	7th March	Return to Lisbon
	1st August to 14th October	**Stay at Queluz**
	1st August	Departure to Queluz
	14th October	"His Majesties and the whole Royal Family went to Ajuda"
	9th November to 15th December	**Stay at Vila Viçosa**
	9th November	"Yesterday morning His Majesties and the whole Royal Family went through Aldeia Galega, from where they will continue their journey until Vila Viçosa."
	11th November	"His Majesties arrived to Vila Viçosa on the night from 11th to 12th November."
	21st November	"the Queen Mother spent some time hunting and killed many animals"
	15th December	Arrival of the royal family to Ajuda (Stay at Vila Viçosa interrupted during Christmas)
1779	**18th January to 9th March**	**Stay at Salvaterra**
	18th January	"in the morning, His Majesties and the Royal Family will take ship and depart to Salvaterra accompanied by a great part of the Court"
	2nd February	"From Salvaterra we get the pleasant news that His Majesties and the Royal Family are in good health. The King Our Lord goes hunting frequently."
	9th March	Return to Lisbon
	1st July to 30th October	**Stay at Queluz-Mafra-Queluz**
	1st July	Departure from Lisbon to "the farm of Queluz, where they intend to spend the rest of the summer"
	5th(?) to 13th October	**Mafra**
	5th October	"His Majesties and the Royal Family are in Mafra"
	13th to 30th October	**Queluz**
	13th October	Return from Mafra to Queluz
	30th October	Return from Queluz to Ajuda
1780	**19th January to 7th March**	**Stay at Salvaterra**
	19th January	Departure of the king and queen to Salvaterra
	15th February	"His Majesties and the Royal Family remain in Salvaterra, benefiting from the small breaks that the continuous rain has allowed."

[1]Information regarding the first semester of 1778 was taken from MMR-28. All other data were gathered from the *Gazeta de Lisboa*.

	7th March	Return of the Royal Family to Ajuda
	23rd June to 22nd August	**Stay at Queluz**
	23rd June	Departure to Queluz
	22nd August to 31st October	**Stay at the Terreiro do Paço**
	22nd August	With the exception of the Widow Queen, the Royal Family went back to Lisbon "and settled in part of the buildings that form the Praça do Comércio, so the King can more easily take the baths of the Alcacerias."
	31st October	His Majesties had dinner in Queluz and from there "went back to the Ajuda Palace, where the Widow Queen and the Infanta D. Maria are expected to return to, coming from Caldas."
1781	15th January	At the age of seventy-two, D. Mariana Vitória, wife of D. José I, dies.
	January to March	**The stay at Salvaterra does not take place. The royal family stays in Lisbon.**
	3rd July to 9th November	**Stay at Queluz-Mafra-Queluz**
	3rd July	Departure to Queluz
	26th August to 13th September	**Mafra**
	26th August	Departure of the royal family to Mafra, "where it intends to stay for some time"
	13th September to 9th November	**Queluz**
	13th September	Return to Queluz from Mafra. "His Majesties and the Royal Family (…) having spent 19 days in this town, some amused themselves in hunting, which, with the excellence of these airs, contributes to their interesting health"
	9th November	"His Majesties and the Royal Family returned to the Ajuda Palace"
1782	**18th January to 3rd March**	**Stay at Salvaterra**
	18th January	Departure from Lisbon to Montijo, and from there to Salvaterra de Magos
	22nd February	In Salvaterra "His Majesties decided to spend some days in Samora"
	3rd March	Return to Lisbon
	17th June to 8th November	**Stay at Queluz-Mafra-Queluz**
	17th June	Departure to Queluz
	26th August to 21st (?) October	**Mafra**
	26th August	Departure to Mafra
	10th September	Stay at Caldas
	21st October	Return from Óbidos to Mafra
	21st October to 8th November	**Queluz**
	21st October	From Mafra to Queluz
	8th November	Departure to Lisbon
1783	**18th January to 11th March**	**Stay at Salvaterra**
	18th January	Departure from Lisbon to Samora
	1st February to 11th March	Stay in Salvaterra
	3rd June to 7th November	**Stay at Queluz-Mafra-Queluz**
	3rd June	Departure to Queluz
	26th August to 22nd September	**Mafra**
	26th August	Departure to Mafra
	22nd September	Return to Queluz
	22nd September to 7th November	**Queluz**
	22nd September	Return to Queluz
	7th November	Departure to Lisbon
		(Continues)
1784	**20th January to 8th March**	**Stay at Salvaterra**

	20th March	Departure to Salvaterra, first passing by Montijo and Samora
	1st February	Arrival to Salvaterra de Magos
	8th March	Departure to Lisbon
	21st June to 12th November	**Stay at Queluz-Mafra-Queluz**
	21st June	Departure to Queluz
	26th August to 9th September	**Mafra**
	26th August	Departure to Mafra
	9th September	Return to Queluz

(continues)

	9th September to 12th November	Queluz
	12th November	Return to Ajuda
1785	**18th January to 3rd March**	**Stay at Salvaterra**
	10th February	Hunt in Santarém
	14th February	Hunt in Samora
	3rd March	Return to Lisbon
	22nd April to 8th June	**Stay at Vila Viçosa**
	8th June	Return to Lisbon
	3rd July to 26th August	**Stay at Queluz-Mafra-Queluz**
	3rd July	Departure to Queluz
	26th August to 9th September	**Mafra**
	26th August	Departure to Mafra
	9th September	Return to Queluz
	9th September to 9th December	Queluz
	9th December	Return to Lisbon
1786	**18th January to 14th March**	**Stay at Salvaterra**
	8th January	Departure to Samora
	1st February	Arrival to Salvaterra. Summer stay with no references to Queluz
	12th September	The Royal Family is in Caldas
	31st October	Return to Ajuda
1787	5th May	Departure from Vila Franca to Caldas. ? Return to Lisbon
	26th June	Departure from Ajuda to the palace at the Praça do Comércio to catch the airs of the sea
	10th September	The Royal Family is in Sintra
	30th October	Return to the palace at the Praça do Comércio
1788	**18th January to 13th February**	**Stay at Salvaterra**
	18th January	Departure to Montijo and afterwards to Salvaterra
	13th February	Return to Lisbon
	5th May to 15th October	**Stay at Caldas-Terreiro do Paço**
	5th May	Departure to Caldas
	4th July	Departure to Terreiro do Paço
	22nd September to 15th October	**Stay at Queluz**
	22nd September	Departure to Queluz
	15th October	Return to Lisbon
1789	**26th January to 6th March**	**Stay at Salvaterra**
	26th January	The royal family went by land to Vila Franca, and from there took a ship to Salvaterra
	6th March	Return to Lisbon
	2nd June	Departure to the Terreiro do Paço
	15th July to 4th November	**Stay at Queluz**
	15th July	Departure to Queluz
	4th November	Return to Ajuda

(Continues)

1790	**19th January to 13th March**	**Stay at Salvaterra**

88

	19th January	Departure to Salvaterra
	13th March	Return to Ajuda
	6th July	Departure to the Terreiro do Paço
	17th August to 12th November	**Stay at Queluz-Mafra-Queluz**
	17th August	Departure(?) to Queluz
	28th August to 14th September	**Mafra**
	28th August	Departure to Mafra
	14th September	Return to Queluz
	14th September to 12th November	**Queluz**
	12th November	Return to Ajuda
1791	**20th January to 16th March**	**Stay at Salvaterra**
	20th January	Departure to Salvaterra de Magos passing through Vila Nova
	16th March	Return to Ajuda
	26th July to 26th August	**Stay at Queluz-Mafra-Queluz Caldas (?)**
	26th August	Departure to Queluz
	26th August to 13th September	**Mafra**
	26th August	Departure to Mafra
	13th September	Return to Queluz
	13th September to 15th November	**Queluz**
	15th November	Return to Lisbon, to Ajuda
1792	**14th January to (?) March**	**Stay at Salvaterra**
	26th March	The royal family stays in Queluz and the *Gazeta de Lisboa* reports the illness of D. Maria I
	11th December	Return to Ajuda
1793	**21st June**	Out and home journey from Queluz to Salvaterra
1794		**Stay at Salvaterra stops occurring**
	30th June to 7th November	**Stay at Queluz**
	30th June	Departure to Queluz
	7th November	Return to Lisbon
	10th November	**Fire at the Real Paço da Ajuda**
	18th November	The royal family has dinner at the Bemposta palace
	November	**The royal family resides in Queluz**
1795		**Residence in Queluz**
1796	**11th January to 14th February**	**Stay at Vila Viçosa**
	11th January	The royal family, with the exception of Queen D. Maria I who stays in Queluz, leaves for Vila Viçosa, passing through Aldeia Galega.
	13th January	Arrival to Vila Viçosa
	22nd January	The royal family makes a tour to Elvas
	23rd January	The royal family makes a tour to Badajoz
	26th January	The kings of Portugal expect the Catholic kings for a hunt in Vila Viçosa
	12th February	Return to Queluz through Évora and Vendas Novas
	12th February	Évora
	13th February	Vendas Novas
	14th February	Arrival to Queluz
1797	**24th to 26th October**	**Occasional journeys from Queluz to Mafra**
1798		**Fixed residence in Queluz**
1799		**Idem**
1800		**Idem**

The summer and autumn stays, from the end of August to the beginning of October, were divided between hunting partridges and chasing deer in the reserves of Belas and Sintra, close to the Palaces of Queluz and Mafra. Sometimes, during the months of October and November, the royal family went to Vila Viçosa, where it extended its stay to hunt deer. By the end of November or beginning of December, it interrupted the hunting stay and returned to Lisbon, where it attended Christmas mass at Court. After Twelfth Night, it started the winter stay in Salvaterra de Magos. During the stay, it went from there to other game reserves, sometimes sleeping in Pancas, Samora or Almeirim. This time of the year was also appropriate to hunt deer, wild boar and other animals[256].

Usually, the return to Lisbon was made during March, at the beginning of Lent. In the capital city, the royal family attended Easter mass and stayed at Court until "Flower Easter", i.e. Whit Sunday. In May or June, after Corpus Christi, it went to the palace of Queluz. From the mid-seventeen eighties of the 18th century, before going to Queluz in May or June, the royal family moved to the Paço da Ribeira, to catch more appropriate airs for the Queen's health, or to Caldas da Rainha, staying there until the beginning of the summer stay at Queluz. The royal family stayed in this palace during a great part of the summer, using the reserves of Belas, Sintra and Lisbon and its surroundings to hunt partridges, until it returned to Mafra by the end of August. In mid-September or the beginning of October they returned to Queluz, where they remained until the end of November or beginning of December. The family then returned to Lisbon, where the cycle started all over again[257].

Annually, in the first fortnight of January, the Surveyor-General received and transmitted orders to the beaters of royal reserves, ordering them to be present at Salvaterra de Magos usually two days before the (anticipated) arrival of the Queen. Beaters came from the different reserves of Salvaterra de Magos, Benavente, Muja, Coruche, Santarém, Almeirim, Samora and Pinheiro[258]. From 1777 to 1786, the full set of summoners, beaters, dog keepers, farm servants, wood keepers and gamekeepers used in royal hunts varied from around 250 to 350[259]. Before the royals arrived, beaters had to clean all the ways through the woods, so that their majesties could easily pass on horseback.

From October to November, on the other hand, wood keepers are ordered to cut down the necessary wood to build bridges and routes in the royal reserves, both in the winter and summer game reserves. D. Maria demanded special care in the treatment of the roads, severely punishing those responsible for their maintenance whenever she detected negligence. In Sintra, in the summer of 1781, the Queen severely rebuked the town's judge because of the slackness of the reserve's ways and the lack of co-operation of the town's officers with the officers of the Surveyor-General's Department. The Reserve Judge of Sintra wrote to the Surveyor-General asking for his word on the procedure of the officers in cleaning the ways. This one, feeling pity for his companion's state of humiliation, declared, "the man became more confused because he had received a public rebuke from the Queen on this regard, as she did not believe the ways were well cleaned when she had come to this land"[260]. Orders to use wood from the royal reserves to repair the ways were given occasionally every two years. No excuses were accepted for the lack of resources or the Surveyor-General's permissions[261].

The Surveyor-General ordered the felling of wood from November to December for the kitchens of "His Majesty" during the winter "royal stay", and from April to May to prepare the kitchen for the summer stays[262]. The register books where entries of supplies and expenses of royal reserves' pantry were recorded also show the regularity in the annual preparation of the royal family's visits to Salvaterra de Magos[263].

When looking at the legislation it can be seen that the Queen regularly signed documents at game reserves. The observation of the places where she signed the diplomas makes one understand that the signatures of documents written in Salvaterra, Queluz and Mafra, generally match the deer and partridge hunting seasons. Ministers went to the palaces where the Queen and D. João VI were staying, so that the monarchs could sign the documents[264].

The royal family could thus enjoy the exclusive use of extensive leisure spaces and their natural resources, but these also become the focus of deep-seated conflicts with those lacking access to the same. Conflicts about resources trigger a variety of crimes exercised "against the reserve" which the Surveyor-General tries to control.

3.3. Social conflicts

Crime inside royal reserves was either through illicit smuggling, which might be opposed by the authorities, or even with the connivance of them. Similarly, poaching was practiced by inhabitants in general, by official hunters of the municipalities, by shepherds and by a significant part of reserve officers, registrars and judges. For rural populations, poaching was either a means of survival and a complement to their agrarian activities or even a "professional" undertaking, well organised both by criminals and reserve guards.

On the other hand, the royal woods also provided a parallel market to buy and sell wood for both charcoal-production factories and other purposes. This market existed because of the perfect articulation between reserve guards and the boatmen who transported the wood outside royal reserves. Wood and undergrowth were also used and traded illegally. Apart from being used to renovate pastures, forest fires were frequently used to make game leave their hiding places so that hunters could kill them more easily.

The mechanism was simple. The master of felling selected the trees to cut down and added a cartload more to the official order sent by the Surveyor-General. Gamekeepers and wood keepers who should survey the felling, as well as the registrar, ignored the trees marked in excess. After the trees had been cut down, they were transported to be shipped in Lisbon, and the boatman "did not care" to take one extra cartload of wood, undergrowth or charcoal. In addition, everything occurred with the most perfect official (il)legality[265]. Conditions were ideal. The reserve guards and registrars who had authorisations and legitimacy to act in the field could easily appropriate goods. In addition, they possessed the necessary means of coercion to "advise" their "partners" in this "parallel commercial activity" not to speak to their superiors.

Royal reserves ended up contributing to the organised smuggling of venison, tanned animal skins and wood. Connivance or the pure inoperativeness of local authorities contributed to the existence of fixed smuggling routes, disturbed by honest and fulfilling officers of the Surveyor-General's Department. Illegal traffic of natural resources was the permanent tragedy of the reserves that the Surveyor-Generals tried to end , almost in vain.

3.3.1. Hunting

Prohibition to hunt in royal reserves, established by the Regulations of the Surveyor-General's Department, was broken regularly on a daily basis. Not even the application of the Regulations of 1775, with which daily and nightly policing during the summer season was reinforced, and the Regulations of 1779, which made inhabitants become watchers, had put an end to the rhythm with which poaching occurred or reduced the frequency of forest fires that devastated the bushes where animals took shelter.

Between 1777 and 1782 references to fires occurring in the summer months are abundant: every two days or, for some periods, daily, with various simultaneous occurrences in the same or in several reserves[266]. Although the policing system of 1779 created by Pina Manique bore some fruit in 1780, complaints from reserve guards, the judges of Santarém and Setúbal and reserve judges, reporting the frequency of fires and their incapability to prevent them within the available means, were frequent. As was frequently the case, the Surveyor-General replied blaming the guards for their incompetence. This situation occurred until the beginning of the French Invasions and after these until the Constitutional Assembly.

In 1777, right after the beginning of his administration, D. Fernando José de Melo tried to reduce the frequency of forest fires, as well as all poaching processes. Pressure from the Surveyor-General on his officers for them to arrest shepherds and poachers who set fires was high. However, to fight back crime it was important to soften the peasants' penalties.

So much was demanded from populations that it is the Marquis of Angeja, minister of D. Maria, himself who, in a document sent to the Surveyor-General, warned, "it is important not to exaggerate on the (penalties) of the Surveyor-General's and reserves' regulations, because if they are too strict they will not be observed. So, it will be enough that the penalty for using burnt lands as pastures one year after the fire be extended for two years"[267]. The minister had understood that in order to get the co-operation of populations it was necessary not to exaggerate penalties. It was important however to stop and punish the criminals who acted daily against reserves.

Following the inquiry into the reserves of Santarém, held in 1777, D. Maria reacted harshly and energetically. According to information gathered, not only had fires not decreased by the end of 1778 but also it was also very difficult to find out who the criminals were. Besides, the inquiry showed that deer and wild boar were frequently hunted in reserves. In 1779, the Queen put back into force the legislation proclaimed in 1752, according to which royal reserves had to be permanently under investigation. In that same year she reinforced the legislation of 1612 for the populations of Aldeia Galega and Benfica do Ribatejo, forbidding the use and possession of weapons inside reserves, which by this time no one obeyed. To obtain results to allow the Surveyor-General's Department to act, she also confirmed the obligation to keep secret the statements of all individuals cross-examined. This measure aimed to encourage inhabitants to reveal criminals, guaranteeing their protection. Otherwise, they would not cooperate because of fear of retaliations from the "horrendous" criminals[268].

The order of secrecy also aimed at putting an end to anonymous accusations, which often served as an instrument for personal revenge among reserve inhabitants and officers. The inquiry on poaching, held in March 1779 at the reserve of Coruche, began because of an accusation, which the accuser refused to sign, for fear of retaliation. After hearing thirty testimonies, it was found that this accusation was irrelevant and that the shepherds accused of shooting a deer were innocent. It was proved that those accused could never have shot the deer because none of them knew how to use guns[269].

Given the general knowledge on the ease with which his majesty's interests could be damaged, in June 1779, the Surveyor-General ordered the judge of Setúbal to begin an inquiry on that circuit court to find out who were the accomplices of the poacher called Alcassereno[270]. We will now examine that document as an example of the illegalities committed in capturing and selling animals in reserves.

With 112 witnesses having been questioned in the Official Inquiry of the "special committee to which presided, under immediate order of Her Majesty, Doctor Bernardino António de Faria e Barros, judge and magistrate of this circuit court and in it commissioner judge in royal reserves, by decree of his Ladyship, of the transgressions performed in those reserves". The guilty ones were found and they were as follows: those who hunted "freely" in royal reserves, those who bought directly from criminals, and "goods' receivers" who sold these in the market.

The investigation occurred *in camera proceedings*. Dr Bernardino de Faria e Barros asked each witness what they knew about the official inquiry, whether they knew the motive for having been called to testify, and what information they could provide on the existence of poachers inside reserves. In particular, the questioning aimed to find the people who bought and sold venison, whether they made it in broad daylight or under cover, and the places where products were traded.

Testimonies revealed that many inhabitants, as well as some orderlies, wood keepers and even priests, took part in that trade with no guilty conscience, considering that "in Borda d'Água, venison was sold freely". Other witnesses gave excuses for having bought venison alleging that they did not know its origin, since it was permitted to slaughter deer in Pancas and four and a half miles around it. Others excused themselves by saying that magistrates, patrol members and clergymen also made it without reserves with regard to the commercialisation of the product. If authorities did nothing to prevent such situations, it would naturally be illicit.

Throughout the interrogation, witnesses presented the names of various possible poachers. In some cases, they confirmed knowing the actions of the individuals arrested and of others who were still going around freely, stating they "saw" or "heard say" that these individuals openly practiced this activity and that "reserved" meat was publicly traded by them.

In an attempt to catch the criminals mentioned in the testimonies, the Surveyor-General D. Fernando, with the help of the Magistrate, developed a "mostly secret" operation to catch them red-handed. The truth was discovered through an ingenious disguise in this operation to "hunt the hunter". A patrol cable of the reserve dressed in civilian clothes went to the market of Lavradio where he bought venison from a recently killed deer directly from the hunter. Then, after being caught red-handed, the hunter was arrested and taken to a boat. This took him to the Moita Prison. In the middle of the trip, however, the prisoner tried to escape. He hit a guard and threw himself into the sea. Nevertheless, he was caught by the patrol cable and driven to the Moita Prison. After this successful operation, the "special committee" for the inquiry carried on with its diligences and, through the determination of the Surveyor-General, the patrol of Salvaterra, together with the one of Benavente, mounted a "night watch" operation, waiting for criminals at the crossroads where hunters "used to pass with venison to be sold in the Lands of the Borda d'Ágoa".

Patrols intercepted a hunter who had "eight quarters of a deer and a fallow deer" and also carried "a rifle loaded with two bullets (...), plus (...) six bullets (...) fifteen small bullets, three quarters of shots, three flints, one of which broken, and three gunpowder charges in a piece of oxen horn". The mission was going very well until the moment the suspect, who was a forester in the town of Moita, alleged his innocence saying he had hunted the animals four and a half miles away from the reserve of Pancas, near a trough for "Pedrogam and Vale de Cabram". Having no proof that the man had hunted in royal reserves, they set him free, but followed him. In addition, that same day the hunter tried to sell the venison at the market of Lavradio, which was inside the perimeter of her majesty's reserves where venison could not be sold; and so he was finally caught red-handed[271].

Encouraged by the results of imprisonments at the Lavradio and Moita, the Magistrate goes on with the Open Inquiry. After questioning fourteen witnesses in August, the Surveyor-General, by order of the Queen, had those investigations officially and publicly stopped. Nevertheless, the Magistrate should proceed with the inquiry, secretly questioning the witnesses. D. Fernando aimed at using this scheme to pacify the hunters who were still going around freely. The Magistrate and the gamekeepers were to act as though the inquiry had already ended, so they could afterwards catch them red-handed. They had already obtained confirmation of the regularity and easiness with which reserve crimes were committed in Samora, Aldeia Galega, Lavradio, Alhos Vedros and Barreiro.

D. Fernando de Melo ordered the judges of Aldeia Galega, Alhos Vedros and Moita to "arrest them in all secrecy and caution", and ordered the judges of the neighbouring villages to be alert, always in the "strictest secrecy", so that no one suspected that the inquiry was still open. Statements from the questionings provided valuable information. Manuel de Sousa, a 40-year-old shoemaker, stated in his testimony that for "more than three years the Cassareiro" sold "venison in town, twice a week" and brought meat to the market-gardener of the kitchen garden of His Excellency the Kingdom's Chief Doorman", Nobleman of the Royal House. In some cases, the steward of that nobleman, Filipe Nogueira, kept part of this meat for himself. Whenever he did not want it, he sold the meat to a soldier of the Prince's Cavalry regiment, Domingos das Amoreiras. Manuel de Sousa also claimed that "this officer went hunting" and the steward of the Kingdom's Chief Doorman skinned the deer and wore "the skins hunted inside royal reserves"! On the other hand, the "skins worn by Filipe Nogueira" were tanned "by a foreigner who had his own house and tanning factory at Ponte da Junqueira".

José da Moita, servant to Father José de São Boaventura, a Secular Canon of São João Evangelista who lived at the Lavradio, informed that the clergyman also transgressed and bought deer and fallow deer to the "Maltese", the one "called Thomaz". In addition, during the "winter of this year until after Carnival", José da Moita had gone "to buy a deer leg sent by his master", the priest. Immediately after having bought it, the witness stated that the Maltese and the priest had gone "to the village's palace to weigh" the piece of meat "and it weighed thirty-two pounds". Besides, José da Moita also informed that, "when he worked at the priest's farm there was a week when everybody ate deer meat" (supposedly from royal reserves, a dish exclusive to the Queen and her guests). However, the list of accusations and information went on.

Poachers even used the name of town officers to be able to escape patrols. At the end of July, José Rodrigues Massareno, from the village of Alcochete, had tried to sell a quarter of a deer without mentioning it was venison. The seaman Manuel, "who had a wine shop", bought it in good faith. Afterwards, José Rodrigues was stopped by the reserve guards and found "with a load he said was for the Chief Doorman's house". "It is not known whether he was speaking the truth" or whether it was just an argument for the patrol to "let him pass through", but the truth is "he passed through"! Even the officers of the Royal House were directly or indirectly implied in the quiet business of illegally hunting large game. However, there was more.

José Pereira, shoemaker, who had only once bought a piece of deer from Alexandre Caramelo, claimed he had done so because "almost everybody in town was doing it". Adding to these testimonies, Alexandre dos Reis, a 55-year-old "seaman", had known "because he heard say"... "that the monks from Arrábida ate deer meat all year long". And an old servant to the town's doctor declared he had heard several passengers of the boat he travelled in say that "deer meat was sold to the public at the town of Lavradio and even at the palace, when the Alcaide was the tenant" (of that town). On the other hand, one of the government's officers, Joaquim Manoel Pereira, testified that, "Miguel sold venison and several people bought it". Another man also confirmed the fact that the Alcaide also took part in this, as well as other town authorities. These included the town's councillor judge and the price-fixer, António de Oliveira de Andrade, a 47-year-old wine merchant who lived at the Gringal farm, close to the surroundings of Almada, and confirmed the sale of deer and fallow deer meat, made from door to door both at the farms and at the town's butcher's. He reported that the "Negrinho" and

"Domingos Caramelo" had gone to that farm to sell venison: overall, António de Oliveira de Andrade had bought 640 oz., as that same meat was being sold "openly in all towns, as well as in Moura, Alhos Vedros, Lavradio and Barreiro, and even at the butcher's shop of Lavradio".

However, poachers did not act alone. They had "smugglers" for this merchandise. Manuel da Cruz, husbandman at the Barra farm, even stated, "because it was public" that "José Rodrigues de Alcassereno and Alexandre Caramelo" sold venison in villages, their smugglers being "Tomas Narigão" and "Manuel Francisco". If the "smugglers" received the meat in secrecy, they had places to prepare it before selling it. António José, oven-keeper, informed that the "servant of the controller Francisco António" from Alhos Vedros, the hunter João Baptista "had salted the venison inside the controller's properties". However (unfortunately), the witness was not aware whether this had been done with the owner's knowledge or not.

Besides incriminating town authorities, poachers who were in prison ended up accusing old colleagues out of personal revenge. An example of this was the rumour set in Lavradio about the accusation Miguel Tavares supposedly had made against Francisco Santa Marta because this one attacked him first. It was later discovered that the aggression had resulted from an argument between the two on the share of profits from selling meat.

After the inquiry was over, the judge confronted both testimonies to look for a result. The conclusions he reached were disastrous for the Surveyor-General's Department. Venison was sold all over the place, inside and outside royal reserves; it was even the local authorities themselves that bought it, without even inquiring into its origin. To make it worse, it was in the houses of distinguished town inhabitants, in secrecy, that the meat was "slaughtered" and prepared to be sold. When hunters were caught with skins or deer meat, they alleged having hunted them at the reserve of Pancas. However, whether or not this was true, the fact is that inside reserves this trade was forbidden. In addition, clearly, no one abided by the law!

Faced by this situation, several hypotheses were presented. Either the guards were conniving, or they ignored the illegality and were very incompetent. Of the 112 people interrogated, only six had claimed not knowing that venison was sold at the palace of Lavradio. On the other hand, the fact that the meat was slaughtered during the night was an indicator that its origin was indeed the royal reserves. The case became even more compromising because the meat was slaughtered in the houses of people belonging to the government or local authorities. If the local authorities of Lavradio, Alhos Vedros and Barreiro were not directly involved in the "supply market", they surely had a passive attitude, not controlling the mechanisms that allowed this free and abundant trade of a kind of meat that should be exceptionally controlled.

Apart from the meat, deerskins were also traded illegally. As well as supplying the meat market, poaching also supplied raw materials for the "tanning factories". Both the inhabitants and the reserve guards had the skins tanned at a reserve away from the one where they had committed the crime of hunting it. Since the process had to be conducted by the judge with jurisdiction on the area where the crime had been committed and no evidence was found, it took some months for the process to be solved. In addition, if game and wood keepers had sent the skins by boat to be tanned in Lisbon, it then took even longer to find who the judge that had to be in charge of this case was. The criminal process could then take up to two years to be started……..time enough for the "criminal" to escape.

In the 1779, at the inquiry of Setúbal the criminal process was clearly indicated. "José Joaquim Franco Moreira, apprentice pilot, 21 years of age, said that Manoel Gonçalves Lobato had had skins tanned in Lisbon and that the person who had brought them was from Aldeia Galega". He also said, "that the soldier from the second company of the Peniche regiment, João António Lopes, knew who tanned skins at Lavradio". The testimony of "António Pereira o Aldagalega, seaman" (mentioned in the process as transporter of skins to be tanned) "did not say a word on the inquiry, but had transported skins from Lisbon" to Aldeia Galega[272].

In sight of these results, the Surveyor-General ordered police reinforcements. Nevertheless, the chasing of hunters and the increase in patrol surveillance inspired the criminals' creativity, making them come up with more elaborate ways to evade police controls. In June 1779, for example, the watchman from the Torre das Cabaças in Santarém invented an instrument that provided better, almost perfect, conditions to commit the crime: a gun easily dismountable. The craftsman built a rifle that could be taken to pieces and put inside a handbag. Patrol guards from Santarém detected this "appalling crime" during a routine operation when they decided to investigate whether the watchman was carrying venison inside his "closed" bag[273].

From 1779 onwards, although inquiries were still "open" and "permanent" at the reserves of Palma, Pinheiro and Santarém, the incapacity to prevent the regular occurrence of reserve crimes went on. Registrars, gamekeepers, reserve judges and their relatives, perpetrated major abuses. The inhabitants accused these of being the main poachers. The inquiry of Benavente, the motive of which was the false accusation of a reserve goat herder of hunting deer with firearms (and we say false because "the hunter is so rude that he cannot even use a gun"), allowed the conclusion that if there was indeed a hunter that hunter was "the reserve's registrar (...) who often goes to the woods alone carrying a rifle"[274].

Warned by the Surveyor-General about this situation, the reserve judge of Benavente began a series of searches of the houses of inhabitants and reserve guards during the months of June and July. The results were devastating as only three rifles were found[275]. Nevertheless, surveillance maintained by his officers was rewarded. On August 9th 1780, the judge Caetano António de Freitas informed D. Fernando that his patrol had arrested a "town's runaway soldier", brother to the "gamekeeper José dos Santos", who when caught was in possession of "two animals" on top of a donkey.

Confirming the ongoing conflict with reserve authorities, an anonymous accusation made on July 17th 1781 accused the reserve judge of Coruche, Apolinário José Nunes, and Fr. Francisco Serrão, priest of that same town, of being poachers, "it is public and notorious in all surroundings of that town that they kill and maintain their houses with deer, fallow deer and boar meat". To make matters worse, according to the accusation, the judge aforementioned also intimidated the Surveyor-General's Department officers with prison penalties, and extorted money out of them.

With poor results in terms of fighting back against reserve criminals, the Surveyor-General sent a warning to the Queen in 1781, stating the measures he thought were necessary to intimidate firearm hunters and fire-raisers. His suggestions resulted in the Edict of February 28th 1781, which granted guards the permission to shoot poachers. Her Majesty ordered now that this edict be sent to the Desembargador António de Melo Ataíde, judge of Santarém, for him to post it all over his territory and in the properties close to reserves and parks. On the other hand, she warned "ministers, judges and authorities of those same towns and places" for them to watch with a lot more care all individuals who appear to be "unoccupied, lazy and having a bad way of living". She ordered them to arrest such individuals, to open verbal proceedings against them, to send them and the summaries of their proceedings to the Police Superintendent, and to put them in the Limoeiro Prison in Lisbon, for the safety of the guards themselves.

The determination of sending hunting criminals to Court followed the complaints presented by the judge of Alcochete, João António Rodrigues de Andrade, "Poachers arrested during the inquiry of 1777 were released from jail by many men"; "after having forced the bars with the help of prisoner José da Cruz", they waited for the officers who conducted the process "and knocked them down (...), one of them is bleeding. (...) the jails of this town have no security whatsoever" and to prevent prisoners from escaping "it would seem convenient that they were sent to the Limoeiro"[276].

In February 1781, 80 edicts were sent to royal reserves and surrounding villages, to be posted by the judges of Santarém, Setúbal and Torres Vedras, magistrates of the districts of Avis and Alenquer, as well as reserve judges, chief game and wood keepers of royal reserves, the Houses of the Infantado and of the Queens.

As one can see in Table 2, the distribution of orders and the care in transmitting the law to all inhabitants, inside and outside reserves, so they cannot "allege ignorance" of the hunting prohibitions inside reserves, shows the Surveyor-General's Department's incapacity to prevent in practice what the regulations proscribed. The vulnerability of reserves stood out both by the distribution of the places where edicts were posted and by the number of edicts sent to each place. In June 1777, three weeks after having been appointed to his post, the Surveyor-General had had only nine edicts sent to reserve judges and chief gamekeepers of the several large game royal reserves. This was an official statement of the then recently appointed Surveyor-General at the beginning of his administration[277]. The need to reinforce that procedure four years later, strengthened with capital punishment, showed how fragile authority was and how ineffective coercive means were in royal reserves.

In spite of the systematic renewal of prohibitions and actions to chase down the illegal hunters and traders, crime against game went on year after year. Although there were increasing number of prisoners caught for hunting crimes or using hunting gear (like powder-flasks or bullets), or for possession of deer meat or deer objects (deer and fallow deer horns), the fact that guards were conniving with poachers was a certainty. Reserve Judges and Chief Gamekeepers frequently complained about this to D. Fernando.

Table 2[278]

Edicts of the prohibition of hunting and setting fire in royal reserves

Posted in 1777 and 1781

	1777		1781
Places	**No. of edicts**	**Places**	**No. of edicts**
		Setúbal	10
		Avis	8
		Alenquer	6
		Torres Vedras	6
Salvaterra	1	Salvaterra	2
Santarém	1	Santarém	4
Almeirim	1	Almeirim	2
Benavente	2	Benavente	3
Coruche	1	Coruche	3
Samora and Belmonte	2	Samora, Belmonte and Pinheiro	3
		Chamusca	3
		Alcácer	3
		Arrábida	3
		Óbidos	3
		Alenquer	2
		Sintra, Colares and New Reserve of Belas	6
		Lisbon and Sítio das Praias (Belém)	8
		Pinheiro	3
		Comporta	2
Muja	1		

In December 1781, the judge of Santarém reported to the Surveyor-General the co-operation of one of his subordinates, the gamekeeper João Frazão Lopes. The gamekeeper had written several times to the judge, informing him of an old and sick prisoner who should be transferred to the hospital so he would not die in prison. Given the gamekeeper's insistence, the judge had consented to inform the Surveyor-General of this case and, with the judge's opinion, D. Fernando had authorised the prisoner's transfer to the hospital. As soon as he got the license to transfer the "old hunter", the gamekeeper João set him free and let him go away.......freely and in good health.

Complicity between criminals and guards was a given. While some operated, seeming to actively co-operate in the protection of reserves, and even deserving a compliment from the reserves' general judge, others limited themselves to not fulfilling their duty. The Surveyor-

General sought to open the eyes of that judge on the guards' good deeds, calling his attention to reality and accusing reserve officers of inaction and negligence: "I who know them best and know they do not care with the fulfilment of their obligations"[279]. Nevertheless, some guards were competent and even defied death when agreeing to meet the poachers who arranged meetings with them in the middle of the night... meetings to which criminals do not go. This was what happened on May 1782 at the reserve of Pinheiro. The gamekeeper António Monteiro had been offended and deceived by poachers who had sent him an anonymous note telling him to meet them, late at night, near one of the woods of that reserve[280]. With the gamekeeper's honour hurt, the Reserve Judge of Salvaterra sent an order to the Wood Keeper of Pinheiro, Pedro Heitor, telling him to find out secretly where the "hunter" lived, as apart from sending an "insulting" note to that gamekeeper he had also not kept his word and had failed to show up. The honour of the Surveyor-General's Department was at stake and it should be restored.

In spite of recurrent failure, sometimes guards succeeded in their watches and managed to catch and arrest some poachers red-handed. Until 1787, the strategy was based mainly on surprise searches, in the houses of reserve inhabitants, especially in Aldeia Galega, Muja, Coruche and Benavente. However, the success of operations rested on the secrecy kept until the moment of action. To avoid leaks of information, not even the guards themselves knew the days when searches were to be made. This way the judges of the reserves of Coruche and Benavente tried to prevent patrol guards from warning inhabitants in time for them to get rid of all the evidence. Mistrust among the Surveyor-General's Department staff was enormous. Besides anonymous complaints by Coruche inhabitants against the performance of game and wood keepers of that town, it was the reserve judge himself who suggested to the Surveyor-General that firearms should only be given to guards during watch periods. The arms would have to be given back to the judge at the end of each shift or extra operation, to be kept in a safe place. Such was the trust the judge had for the guards he led! The Surveyor-General agreed and this rule remained in force until the French Invasions, and was reinstated in the period following the Constitutional Assembly.

Between 1782 and 1787, D. Fernando tried to discipline his officers' behaviour through consecutive intimidation and constant demand for results from the inquiries, especially in large game reserves. However, no matter how many watches the guards made, and seizure of guns and hunting equipment, crimes did not decrease. Not even the sudden searches made of several reserve villages had much effect. From 1782 onwards, D. Fernando de Melo ordered the arrest of all dogs inside royal reserves if their owners did not possess licenses to raise them. Those animals kept for the royal packs were maintained but the others were to be slaughtered[281]. In any of these circumstances, dogs were always be taken from their owners. The indicators that there were dogs on the loose in royal reserves were the bitten, wounded or dead deer that guards found on the ground. Most of them had managed to escape hunters' persecution after having been bitten by their dogs[282]. Whenever guards found deer wounded by dogs or by the nets protecting arable fields they were bound to report it to the Surveyor-General. They did not always report these occurrences, however, and kept the meat for themselves instead of arresting the alleged criminals. The gamekeeper of Samora and Belmonte was arrested for three days for "having apprehended a wounded fallow deer" instead of arresting the individual who was stood over the animal[283].

On May 18th 1787, to ease the capture of animals reserved for His Majesty's pleasure, the new Surveyor-General D. Francisco de Melo ordered the start of inquiries in all game reserves and surrounding districts. In the same diploma, he established the "fencing" of royal reserves, as already noted in Chapter 1.1.2. These measures aimed to make daily and nightly summer watches more effective. From 1775, these were made with the help of detachments of cavalry soldiers. In this way D. Francisco de Melo informed the authorities of the reserves' towns of the importance of the regulations. The towns were Santarém, Almeirim, Alpiarça, Benfica, Coruche, Erra, Montargil, Lamarrosa, Muja, Salvaterra, "and the towns which, however not reserved, are neighbours to those", Aveiras de Cima, Aveiras de Baixo, "Azambuja of the Santarém district" and Galveias, belonging to the district of Avis[284]. Since until then, the policing measures adopted in reserves had limited results, the Queen spread the net of intimidation to a larger number of villages outside reserves but close to them.

Throughout the whole period during which they administered reserves Surveyor-Generals were very strict on a judicial level but benevolent towards "reserve criminals" who, because of their level of "misery", are worthy of "royal mercy". D. Fernando José de Melo was very careful to follow the order of procedure to judge an alleged criminal, an attitude that was followed by his successors.

Although the evidence of a crime had been established, if this offence was not witnessed, the alleged criminal was never condemned without convincing evidence. Groundless accusations, due to malicious accusations between goat keepers or between inhabitants, sometimes hid the fact that the accused was after all innocent. Therefore, to put a process under way the first thing to do, was to start interrogating witnesses and suspects. If these were considered innocent, they were released. Often, even when they were proclaimed guilty, if the hunters were very poor farmers with a wife and children, or if they were very old, they were favoured with royal pardon. When the real "hunting criminals", i.e. the individuals who usually make hunting in royal reserves their profession, were caught however, justice was tough. Whenever possible, prisoners were sent to the Limoeiro Prison to be judged there by the judge of the High Court, general judge of reserves. Penalties applied even included deportation to India.

From 1787 to 1789, D. Francisco José Luís de Melo followed his father's policy. From his appointment in 1789 onwards, D. Francisco da Cunha, cousin to D. Francisco José Luís de Melo, followed the policy of his immediate predecessors, insisting his officers fulfil their functions. Along with showing he would not simply threaten to arrest criminals but he intended be successful in doing this, he began investigations into the trespasses and poaching of his officers. In July 1789 the wood keeper of Samora was arrested for having taken the day off to "go hunt mallards" at the fen of Pera and Comporta instead of giving the duly assistance to fight wolves at the reserve[285]. In addition, showing his commitment in imposing authority, in the following five years he obtained improved results. This was shown by the yearly transport of prisoners to Lisbon.

Between March 1794 and July 1795, the period during which D. Francisco was called to take part in war; D. Luís Pinto de Sousa replaced the Surveyor-General in office. He tried to follow D. Francisco's guidelines but his results were less clear. The network of complicities between representatives of the law and criminals continued and in 1795 the reserve judge of Benavente and Salvaterra reported to D. Luís the escape of the criminal Cláudio Manuel, a "terrible offender" and "aggressor of royal reserves who had often relapsed. By forcing the jail open, he had once again committed crimes with help inside and out; he absconded by filing through the iron chains around his feet and escaping. The judge's response was to arrest the warden, who was accused of the "omission of not verifying the prisoner's chains every evening"[286].

Back from war in 1795, D. Francisco found the reserves once again in chaos. Besides, having been moved to Tavira as Governor of Arms of Alentejo, it was from there that he conceived the plan to reorganise the reserves. With a clear vision of events, he recognised the evidence that in royal reserves, given the dimension of reserves and the number of officers available, the control of crime was impossible. Without other resources, however, D. Francisco da Cunha once again repeated the prohibitions for all inhabitants established in reserves. These included the possession of firearms for those living up to four and a half miles away from the reserve. Any hunter who transgressed this rule was in danger of being "reputed as poacher in those reserves" and punished as such. The only exception foreseen consisted in the permit granted to those who needed to use the reserve's roads. Nevertheless, they were bound to "go through those roads (…) with no gunlocks in their rifles"[287].

As the forest continued to decrease at a constant rate it was necessary to protect game and tree species useful for the royal household. The Surveyor-General understood that, for example, he could not force either the communities or the guards to fight back forest fires. Trying to get around this situation, D. Francisco changed his strategy. To the punitive message, he added penalties in cash collected to all disobedient persons, officers and inhabitants of the villages inside the reserves. In a letter on September 28th 1798, sent to the Reserve Judge of Benavente and Salvaterra, he announced strong measures to be applied to all those who refused to firefight with individual penalties of $300 *reis*. Although threatened through these methods, local people still shunned the task and were indifferent to officers' warnings and threats. In addition, as with the strongly punitive measures adopted by D. Fernando and D. Francisco de Melo, the actions of D. Francisco da Cunha were shown to be insufficient.

However, the Surveyor-General was persistent, and brought in new ways to combat poaching. Instead of capturing poachers on the ground, he tried to find out who in the tanning factories were the ones having skins tanned. This was possible because the names of all individuals who sent skins to tan were inscribed in the factories' register books. This new approach was very successful.

On October 20th 1799 the Surveyor-General wrote to the Reserve Judge of Muge asking him to observe the tanning factories, and the searches made during August brought good results: 58 skins and 13 rifles were apprehended[288]. He ordered this approach to go on with the arrest of all tanning factory managers who do not make their register books available.

From the reform of royal reserves' regulations by the decree of March 21st 1800 onwards, and until the French Invasions, steps such as the reduction of reserved areas and the reform of patrolling, now made on horseback, seemed to work. The inclusion of Pancas in the group of reserves policed by the Surveyor-General's Department put an end to the existence of an "island" where poachers acting inside reserves, and allowed improved policing of those same reserves. On the other hand it opened a conflict between the Crown and the owners of Pancas.

The property of Pancas had been established as an inalienable property and hunting reserve in the 15th century and its limits could not be changed. Having the law on his side, the Lord of Pancas appealed to justice for all his rights on the reserve to be returned. However, still without success in the legal process, he died in 1802, leaving no direct heirs. The property right to Pancas was inherited by the niece of the former owner and not by the widow, D. Maria Balbina. The latter felt offended and filed a lawsuit against the niece and her husband, D. José de Oliveira e Daun. She stated that the property was handed over by the Duke of Bragança, the alleged assassin of D. João II, to whom the entailed interest of Pancas belonged in the 15th century. In this case, the estate should have passed to the hands of the Crown, because its owner had committed high treason and ever since then the property had been wrongly in the hands of his heirs.

With this argument, D. Maria Balbina wished to delay the delivery of the accounting books of the house to the landlord of Pancas. D. José de Oliveira's lawyer presented a counter-argument based on the evidence presented by the accuser against the Crown at the time of the inclusion of Pancas in the regulations of royal reserves. However, the process was dragged out through the courts. In 1809, when D. José took part in the delegation sent to Bayonne to meet Napoleon, the process was still unresolved.

In 1811, D. José tried to regain his property since the argument of the crime of high-treason invoked by D. Maria Balbina was unconvincing. The pretext invoked to disentail that property from his house had been an unfair accusation of treason whilst he was participating in the Bayonne delegation. Meanwhile, in 1810, by judicial ability or the will of the King, Pancas was firmly included as one of the royal reserves, regardless of the arguments[289].

Between 1800 and 1808, apart from the Pancas issue, transgressions in reserves continued. On August 26th 1805, an inquiry began and found the guards of the reserves of Belas guilty. Not only did they police the reserves, but they were also found to "hunt partridges, and with a rifle!" Their guilt having been proved, one year later, the guards were suspended from their duties. On August 28th 1806, the judge of Oeiras was ordered to arrest the guards of the reserve of Sintra. He answered on September 6th saying he could not do it because the two guards lived in areas outside his jurisdiction; one in the surroundings of Sintra and the other in the district of Belas. On October 8th the Judge of Sintra informed the Surveyor-General that he did not arrest them because he could not find where they lived[290].

With the French Invasions, general crimes on reserves increased, making it almost impossible to hold back the hunters who treated royal reserves as free property available to all. However, particularly in Lisbon and its surroundings, the Surveyor-General tried to maintain a degree of effectiveness, at least in terms of partridges. To give substance to these actions and to impose authority, D. Pedro da Cunha had warnings fixed on all reserves informing that, in spite of the King's absence and his stay in Brazil, reserves were not extinct. It was with clear indignation that the Surveyor-General noted the destruction of the pigeon houses of Salvaterra during the occupation of Junot's army. This was following the "strange abuse with which evil-intentioned people dared to destroy the pigeon houses of that same falconry with the slaughter of pigeons thought to be extinct. That unfortunate boldness deserves some serious demonstration, not because of the importance of the slaughter, but because of the irreverence or attack perpetrated to the royal authority, which still has not charged the public with the responsibility of extinguishing its pigeons. This is why, in name of the royal service" D. Pedro recommended that the Judge of Salvaterra imprison the accomplices and find detailed information on the operations[291].

Between 1809 and 1811, in spite of the Surveyor-General's Department's efforts, nothing could be done against an armed population hunting in groups inside royal reserves. The Surveyor-General tried to lessen the chaotic situation of royal reserves and at least manage to keep partridges to be sent to Rio de Janeiro. However, with no effective means at his disposal and his authority exhausted, D. Pedro da Cunha tried one last attempt to accomplish that mission. He ordered the wood keeper of the reserve of Lisbon and surroundings to confiscate partridges "raised in cages" by private owners and "please tell them on my behalf that it would be of royal satisfaction for them to renounce this time to their appetite and make H.R.H.'s pleasure. I have reasons to believe your good diligence, as well as the Portuguese patriotism"[292].

However, not even the appeal to "Portuguese patriotism" solved the problem of protecting partridges and reserves. Resources were scarce and the Surveyor-General could not implement the policing of reserves. Not only did D. Miguel Pereira Forjaz not send him any soldiers to defend them, but additionally, troops were taking part in the crimes of hunting inside royal reserves. In Sintra they even attacked the reserve guards[293]. From 1812 onwards, D. Pedro would have to deal with another problem: British troops in the territory. Several times, between 1812 and 1821, he wrote to Beresford to inform him that the soldiers of British companies, quartered in Lisbon and cantoned or accommodated in Salvaterra, Santarém and Sintra, actively hunted in royal reserves. The British officer's invariable answer was that he would investigate the crimes and punish the criminals, agreeing, on May 1812, to forbid his subordinates to hunt there.

The order transmitted to Colonel Brewan, "Commander of the Deposit of Salvaterra", declared that "no officer of any rank can kill game at the reserves of H.R.H.". Beresford confirmed the exclusive of granting hunting licenses to the Surveyor-General, exception made to "the people whom I would grant a license and also the most honourable Marshall General Count of Vimioso, in case he passed by"[294]. Beresford suggested that, "in no way those employed in guarding reserves should kill game of any sort, as officers should then have a motive to find the difference strange".

In the following year, the Surveyor-General insisted that British high ranking officers control their troops, since he had been told that several "British" officers "presenting themselves with rifles and dogs at the reserve, in the surroundings of this town, not only hunted partridges but also attacked the guards who tried to stop them"[295].

During 1812 and 1813, following his attempt to stop the plundering of reserves, D. Pedro continued sending letters, either to D. Miguel Pereira Forjaz or to Beresford, asking them to help him police reserves with a contingent of the army. However, the answer he got from both is the order to give the Secretary of War and the army's commander the list of reserve employees, so that they could evaluate the elements of the Department that could be included in the army or in the militias.

In this game of forces between the several military bodies, the Count of Castro Marim tried to protect his troops under the royal orders demanding the maintenance of a body of guards to protect reserves. In a letter from October 9th 1813, D. Pedro explained to the Count of Trancoso the need for his officers not to be incorporated. He also demanded explanations for "the fact that, as I have reported to Your Excellency on my letter from the 22nd of last month, the decrees with which some served this office as substitutes and supernumeraries are caught and gathered; and being above all destitute of means to fulfil my obligations, not having officers whom I can entitle for the service of royal reserves, as the owners are not enough, nor capable, as I mentioned to Your Excellency; and besides being few, most of them are old and ill; preserving my responsibility; I beg Your Excellency for instructions or for an answer to my previous letter which I have not yet received"[296]. Five days later, D. Pedro received news that he had won one of the battles. The Chief Gamekeeper of Odemira, Manuel Fogaça de Vasconcellos, was sent back to the Surveyor-General's Department without being incorporated in the militias, "since he had been appointed chief gamekeeper of Odemira before being appointed officer of that body"[297].

In spite of the immense difficulties in managing the Surveyor-General's Department, from 1815 onwards, progress was made. With the population being relatively unarmed and with guilty farmers, guards and Reserve Judges being imprisoned, little by little the Surveyor-General returned some discipline back to royal reserves. This may even have been a little excessive, as in the performance of guard João Viana in 1820. Too zealous to fulfil his obligations, this guard had a man stop who was passing by on the way close to the reserve of Belém and carrying a gun on his shoulder. Since João Viana was carrying no insignias, the plaintiff did not obey him and was then savagely attacked by the guard. After being released, Sebastião Pedro Paulo filed a complaint against the guard of the Coutada Velha (old reserve),

João Manuel Pereira Viana, accusing him of having attacked him and put him in prison, thus abusing his authority. The plaintiff was coming from Benfica, going from his father's house to his own, following a public road by the way that passes close to the old reserve of Belém, when a cloaked individual with no identification whatsoever had stopped him and demanded the gun he was carrying on his back. Not being able to recognise the guard, and given the way this one presented himself, Sebastião refused to give him his rifle. In view of this refusal, the guard attacked him, took away his gun, broke it and "knocked him down with it". Afterwards he had another officer called and put Sebastião in prison.

After leaving jail, Sebastião demanded recompense for the action, both for the excesses committed and by the fact that he was put in jail without having committed any crime. Not only could his rifle not be fired because it had no flint, but he also was walking outside the reserve. Besides, he could not possibly have recognised the officer. In addition, he demanded that the legitimate authority should not become illegitimate by abusing power. He also warned of the dangers that such actions bring, "those authorised by Your Excellency to guard reserves, exceeding the limits of their authority, insult, arrest and ill-treat those who, without offending reserves, walk on the roads that divide them and cut and give free passage to all kinds of people, being sure that the abuse of jurisdiction is an evil with terrible consequences, as it inverts public order and transforms the dispositions of legitimate authorities; also being sure the excesses committed by guard João Manuel Pereira Viana are fully proved in the justification enclosed; and finally being sure that that same guard is scandalous in his behaviour as guard and as private person and that the result of his bad habits, bad inclination and terrible conduct was insulting the plaintiff, arresting him, taking away his rifle, breaking it, and giving him many blows with it. Therefore, does the criminal appear in front of Your Excellency where the truth should never fail as it did.

Thus, the plaintiff appeals to Your Excellency, asking for your unchangeable justice, so that in favour of it Your Excellency finds a solution, ordering as pleases you. Let from it result the release of the plaintiff from that guard's punishment, the amendment of the damage regarding the value of the rifle the mentioned guard made useless, and afterwards was sawn in consequence of the false representation he presented to Your Excellency."

During the 1820s, hunting in the "former royal reserves" cannot easily be assessed since from February 8th 1821 the hunting of noble animals became a right of citizenship. However, in private reserves the absence of policing led to "tax-free" hunting[298].

In conclusion, one can say that the management of hunting between 1777 and 1824 was characterised by continual confrontation between the Surveyor-General's Department's authorities and the communities living inside and outside reserves. Conflicts arose around the hunting of deer and, whilst the Surveyor-Generals were characterised by a serious commitment to defending reserves, policing was limited.

The analysed sources did not allow the discovery of exact figures on the decrease of hunting crimes with the ending of the French threat. However, it is clear that between 1815 and 1817, there was some reinforcement of the authority of the Surveyor-General's Department, the imprisonment and dismissal of corrupt officers, and their replacement by competent guards and magistrates. Although poaching continued from 1816 onwards until the Constitutional Assembly, the correspondence on crimes slows down in comparison to that sent almost daily during the reign of D. Maria and until the French Invasions.

3.3.2. Undergrowth and timber

As with game species, trees, shrubs and pasture resources were preserved within a framework of restrictions on use by the people residing inside reserves. However, these measures threatened the survival of communities who depended on the landscape resources. They were forbidden to use products other than what was allowed for agriculture.

As mentioned in Chapter 2, farming areas were confined to the lands where they did not harm game or the production of timber. As for livestock, the number of swine that could be raised in the sheds was defined by the Regulations of 1605 with measures to avoid cross-breeding of wild boar and "domestic swine" which "makes a lot of damage to wild ones". This was an attempt to maintain the breed of game species as pure as possible[299]. Raising goats was also limited by the prohibition of using royal pastures. To have access to pastures, goatherds set fires but the raising of goats was made difficult by the systematic prohibition to use pastures after a fire. This strategy, used as a measure against forest fires, itself generated problems. In revenge, peasants, goatherds or shepherds intentionally set the woods on fire.

Certainly, in some cases, the fire was the result of ill-controlled ground clearances. However, for the authorities, fires presumably set deliberately (as happened in most cases), were sufficient motive to start an inquiry. This process of investigation involved an inquiry and home searches[300].

Illegal use of royal pastures happened during the whole period studied, and the boldness of goatherds increased from the French Invasions onwards. The Surveyor-General reacted against this abuse by ordering the Chief Wood Keeper, in November 1814, to apprehend all licenses for pastures and "losing no more time have collect and send me those licenses, in case they exist, never giving consent without a written order by this Surveyor-General's Department for goats to go on pasturing inside royal reserves, whatever the motives for their permission or concealment"[301]. This measure did not have the necessary force, but once again was reinforced by the prohibition of "cattle and swine in royal reserves in 1816 and 1818"[302].

Protection to woodland and game species restricted farming in royal reserves. Restrictions were imposed on access to undergrowth and timber, resources used in the daily lives of local people and this worsened their living conditions. On the other hand, wood and timber to repair or make fences for sheds were precious goods for rural communities. This was the only way to both prevent animals from escaping and protect arable fields from damage by large game. Given the importance of this resource for the survival of rural populations, local and departmental authorities were in dispute over who held the legitimacy to grant licenses to fell wood (for sheds, boats and other constructions), to clear grounds by fire (for the soil to be treated and pastures to be renovated), and to build charcoal-production factories[303].

These disputes were frequent between the Administrator of Samora Correia, the Judge of Setúbal and the Surveyor-General, from 1777 to 1781; between the Judges of Óbidos, Benavente and Coruche and the Reserve Judges of Óbidos, Salvaterra, Muge, Chamusca, Coruche, Erra and Benavente throughout this whole period[304]. Restrictions to these activities generated "natural prevarication" and parallel economic activities like illegal timber smuggling. This was made by those having direct and legal access to resources and dominating the mechanisms of power: the felling masters, farm managers, wood keepers, and magistrates.

Traffic circuits and nets were used for game smuggling. At the quays, boats were loaded with extra cartloads of timber and wood and everybody gained from that. The beneficiaries included the boat's master, the master of felling, the wood keeper who watched over felling, and the chief gamekeeper who did not control the wood keeper.

At the reserve of Alcácer, as reported by the Chief Wood Keeper Miguel Ferreira Dias to the Surveyor-General, there was no control or surveillance whatsoever on the activity of wood felling at the quays. The web of complicities in wood smuggling passed, in this case, by the Wood Manager Joaquim Soares Ferrão, by the Master of Felling José Feliciano, and by the Masters of the "ferries". They all cut down woods indiscriminately, without asking for the necessary permits to the "district's" Judge. This one is "offended" and "everybody loses respect for the authority". The boats' master was "instructed" by the wood manager, who "has been abusing and carrying" the cartloads of wood and logs "how and whenever he wishes to", "which clearly shows that in this process the royal treasury may well be damaged, because the masters, having no one to watch over them, can take as much wood as they want"[305].

Inquiries made of the officers of the Surveyor-General's Department reported this very fact. In 1778, at the reserve of Arrábida, a prosecution was set against the Wood Keeper and the reserve's Bailiff for felling wood (and hunting) clandestinely. In 1779, the inquiry of Setúbal, especially intended for reserves' members and inhabitants at the reserves of Palma and Pinheiro, extended to the whole district. In 1781, the reserves of Pera and Comporta were subject to an inquiry into the excessive wood felling, as the Wood Keeper and the Master of Felling were under suspicion. In 1789, another inquiry was set up into the felling of trees at Óbidos, where the reserve's Chief Gamekeeper was under suspicion for negligence. Once again at Óbidos, in 1789, another inquiry was established on the reserve for "improper" felling of poles[306].

At the wood reserves along the coast, away from the place of residence of the Surveyor-General and consequently away from the strict control of the senior hierarchy, abuse of power by the Department's officers against communities and against the Crown was relatively easy. This was particularly the case at the reserve of Óbidos. D. Francisco José de Melo suspected such traffic in tree products, made by his officers, that, in a letter from September 23rd 1799, he sent an order to the Judge of Muja to proceed with surveillance at the

Pinewood of Escaroupim He was to use other assessors not belonging to the reserve of Benavente[307]. With this, the Surveyor-General intended to confirm the truth or otherwise of the deposition of the Benavente Magistrate. Was this definite evidence of D. Francisco da Cunha's suspicion of his officers? Yes, it was. Knowing the difference in depositions but not being able to prove who was guilty, the Surveyor-General sent a report to his Royal Highness warning him about the destruction of the pinewood and asking the King to reduce the number of licenses to cut down wood and to exercise stricter control over the pinewood's dilapidation[308].

Through the whole period analysed, there was a permanent conflict over the reserve of Óbidos between the Surveyor-General's Department's officers and territorial Judges, and between reserve inhabitants and the Department. On August 2nd 1781, the Judge of Óbidos informed D. Fernando de Melo that the Chief Gamekeeper of that reserve was incompetent and dishonest. Not only had he incorrectly marked the logs felled to be granted to a farmer from Alenquer who had asked for them for his shed, but he had also sold wood useful to "royal service"[309]. In 1786, the issue between the municipality's magistrate and the reserve's officers goes on, resulting in the dismissal of the Reserve Judge and the gamekeeper for disrespect, smuggling, abuse of power and corruption. Acknowledging the accusations that the Judge of Óbidos had presented against the Reserve Judge Jerónimo Vaz, D. Fernando sent a first "immediate prison order" "to the Reserve Judge and the Gamekeeper" Francisco Leal, under the accusation of "calling up to himself the office of that same judge, office which, as I was told, is in power of someone whom without permission that judge appointed as registrar of the mentioned reserve". In this office, only "legal" operations were registered, being suppressed or erased the elements that could compromise the Magistrate, the Gamekeeper and the Registrar. In addition, as the Judge of Óbidos had no jurisdiction over the Reserve Judge, he could do nothing but send an accusation to the Surveyor-General for this to act according to his statute[310].

In 1795, the Judge of Óbidos informed the Surveyor-General that "the reserve's ministers scare the farmhands in such a way that they no longer wish to live there" and not even under threat do they agree to fight back forest fires[311]. On January 21st 1798, the Surveyor-General demanded the same magistrate summon the Reserve Officers residing in Óbidos "in 30 days' time" "because their absence and neglect" turned the reserve into a "duty-free" space[312].

From 1800 onwards, the interpretation of the Regulations allowed a series of abuses from all social classes. In 1803, the Surveyor-General was confronted by the inhabitants of Cantanhede, whose woods were policed by the Gamekeepers of Óbidos who claimed for themselves the right to freely cut down timber and undergrowth in the woods of the reserve of Óbidos, apparently unreserved by the Regulations of 1800. On the other hand, in Cantanhede licenses to cut down wood granted to the Count of Bobadela and the Confraria do Santíssimo Sacramento of Óbidos had been passed by "a judge de vara branca" of the *Desembargo do Paço*. The confrontation between jurisdictions was now at the level of the courts of Court.

Rectifying the court's action and believing the law-breakers had acted in good faith, the Surveyor-General had the felling stopped, "being passed the necessary orders so that the precise definition of everything that was cut down within the limits of royal reserves is done, even though the owners are private people" like the Count of Bobadela and the Confraria of Óbidos[313].

Besides officers and the local community, private owners also committed occasional acts, innocent wrongdoing or intentionally and in bad faith. It must be noted that in 1801 all royal reserves and surrounding municipalities had been enlightened on the contents of the new Regulations[314].

From the French Invasions onwards, Portuguese, French and British troops, quartering by the rivers and margins of royal reserves, together with the lack of personnel to control reserves, contributed to the parallel trade in timber. Army officers, both Portuguese and British, stationed at Salvaterra, had timber cut down and sent them to Lisbon. Being armed, they acted with full impunity.

The Surveyor-General was aware of the case of the Salvaterra patrol and wrote a letter to the Count of Linhares warning him of this fact. On January 27th 1812, he sent a letter to Admiral Berkley asking him to punish the British officers who dealt in wood from the reserves[315]. The British Admiral replied promptly, vaguely informing, without mentioning names, that he was investigating those who committed such crimes. The answers concluded that the control of the waters of Ribatejo did not belong to the war navy. Because of this, the authorities of those districts would be the ones having to investigate the origin of the guilty and mete out their punishment according to the country's law. Responsibility given back to the Portuguese and

Portuguese authorities, the action of British officers was reduced to an attempt of moving the guilt from the subjects of His British Highness[316]. In short, what was previously done by the corrupt officers of the Surveyor-General's Department was now continued both by them and by British troops.

However, faced by the need for undergrowth and for timber to supply headquarters, the Surveyor-General co-operated. He granted licenses to fell wood, as long as the soldiers guaranteed that they would not damage the reserves. In the face of General Blunt's promise to "promptly punish (...) any kind of excess" from his soldiers, D. Pedro ordered Lisbon's Patrol Corporal not to prevent cutting of undergrowth by members of the British detachment quartered in Alcântara. He was to allow them to "cut down and take away from that reserve the necessary poles for them to make brooms"[317].

From 1815 onwards, with Napoleon's defeat and the guarantee of peace in Europe, Department officers who had been incorporated into the army or in the militias returned home. The number of officers available to carry out watches increased compared with the period from 1808 until 1814. This facilitated the restart of the combat against criminals, since with policing capacity increased to remedy and prevent abuses that had been encouraged by the war[318].

From 1815 onwards, the Surveyor-General's Department developed the re-establishment of authority and intervention in the field, which seems to be back in place in 1818 with management back to normality. The guards policed the reserves, watched over felling, and, whenever doubts arose, stopped wood cutting. They had to control pasture areas, mark down "dead and sick trees, turning them into charcoal"[319]. They also had to choose the areas where farmers could cut down undergrowth "for household use"[320]. In spite of this, annual, deliberately set criminal fires continued.

With the extinction of royal reserves and of the Surveyor-General's Department in 1821, game and wood reserves of the House of Infantado were no longer protected by a military body. Having more freedom than ever, poachers profited from hunting animals in those reserves and starting fires with impunity. The latter was to drive game out into the open. This catastrophe extended to the reserves of Pancas and the wood reserves of Palma and Pinheiro: "I am informed that some fires have been raised by the hunters and that the officers are not capable of opposing them, as the fires occurred are in great number"[321].

In 1821, there were still prosecutions begun in 1815 relating to the debts of reserve officers to the Surveyor-General's Department for wood purchases between 1807 and 1815. In July 1821, the issue of the Reserve Corporal, José Maria de Vasconcelos, of Samora was still unsolved. He had bought "60 cartloads of wood" and paid for only 40.

CONCLUSIONS

In Portugal, royal reserves present a multi-faceted structure with striking implications in Ancient Regime society. These are both at the level of the definition of monarchy's status and *ethos* and at the level of institution formation and intermediate powers. At the same time, they serve as a barometer of local authorities' respect or disrespect from the crown's authority.

The reserve was a complex unity of restrictions to the use of natural resources, be them game, pastures or forest products. However, the collection of forest and woodland goods was a natural right of the local communities and during the medieval period the reserve system came to limit these. The contestation of space and resources was a systematic point of discussion between the reserve's owner, its inhabitants and external visitors who did not live inside the boundaries. During the Ancient Regime, that right was recognised outside reserves, although the appropriation of resources was regulated by general legislation, municipal bylaws and customs. The reserve system gave rise to one of the most oppressive forms of seigniorial regimes, the creation of a reserve being a royal exclusive and holding it was a privilege of high-rank.

As a symbolic space and the visible manifestation of royal privileges, game reserves acquired a special status. For around five centuries, they constituted one of the places in the kingdom most frequented by the royal family and *the* visible space of permanence of the monarchy. Socially differentiated rituals and techniques associated with hunting and game were simultaneously the elements of identification and distinction of the different social levels. Game reserves and game practice were understood as structuring elements of the aristocratic *ethos*, mainly visible in the *modus vivendi* of Ancient Regime nobility[322]. It was also in game reserves that the Crown granted minor officers, like Game and Wood Keepers the ability to apply capital punishment to transgressors, usually an exclusive right of the King.

On the other hand, along with the Crown's mark of power, wood reserves had a very precise economic role. Royal reserves imposed and perpetuated the reserve system in private woods, making it impossible even for important titleholders and other owners to have access to undergrowth and timber. Royal reserves followed an economic exploitation model aimed at the preservation of reserved resources and the satisfaction of the needs of rural populations living within them. In this sense, reserves were composed of different sections of forest, dense woods, moors and farming areas with distinct purposes. The Surveyor-General's Department's role consisted mainly in protecting game and forest resources from poaching and the advancement of allotments for agriculture and pasturing. Game and Wood Keepers were to select the spaces and resources to be felled, providing rural communities with the necessary forest products for their farming and cattle rearing.

Besides overseeing and allocating areas for different uses, the Surveyor-General's Department also supervised royal reserve exploitation systems. These had two distinct models: 1) direct and 2) indirect exploitation, direct through the Department and indirect through leaseholds and lettings by lease. In private lands within the perimeter of the reserve the formula of exploitation was determined by their landlords[323]. As the destruction of the natural forest area progressed, the strategy to preserve royal reserves and the King's goods required the prohibition of renewed or new lease contracts. This was necessary to release land in part from agrarian uses. From 1800 onwards, fee-farm use was avoided in order to maintain the geographical area of the royal reserves.

During the last quarter of the 18th century, the Royal Academy of Sciences had defended the abolition of reserves, as these constituted an obstruction to agriculture. However, the prohibition of fee-farm contracts did not aim to oppose the growth of agrarian development, on the contrary. The intention was to reduce royal reserved areas and then use available unreserved areas for agricultural purposes. In 1800, the reduction of reserves constituted the practical application of that agrarian tendency. An example was the turning of the reserve of Almeirim, located in the marshy lands of the Tejo, into an unreserved area. This promoted agriculture in those lands. The end of fee-farm contracts, on the other hand, aimed to prevent the alienation of the Crown's own property.

Royal game reserves needed to be managed as an exclusive space of the sovereigns and the royal family. Licenses for large game could only be granted by kings and queens, excluding even the Surveyor-General. Except for members of the royal family, no one could hunt in royal reserves, or in reserves watched by the guards of the Surveyor-General's Department, like the reserves of the Infantado and the House of Queens, without an express permit from the King. Even in the districts of Estremadura, at the reserves of Belém, Alcântara, Necessidades, Ajuda, Belas and Colares, Vila and Serra de Sintra, the Duke of Cadaval, among others, was bound to confirm with the Surveyor-General the hunting permit granted by the King. However, Crown holders and their servants (by order of their masters) frequently broke the law in royal reserves. This was especially in the improper use of royal pastures. Throughout the whole period studied, the Surveyor-General's Department had to face the pressure of the House of Cadaval, the Council of Queens, the administration of Pera and Comporta and Samora. These frequently tried to overcome the Department's jurisdiction and use royal reserves without abiding by their regulations.

Conflicts in royal reserves did not result from a specific political context or from a revolutionary movement. The reserve system that opposed the natural right of the peoples was so violent that by the end of the Ancient Regime it was already questioned[324]. From the Crown's point of view, these ideas were criminal acts and gave origin to inquiries on the game reserves of Pera and Comporta, Alcácer and Santarém. The abolition of reserves was acknowledged as one of the vital points of dispute and liberation of populations during the liberal revolutions in Europe.

There are many testimonies to the misery to which inhabitants were subject and pardons granted for crimes committed by the poor "worthy of royal mercy". These show, in several cases, the disputes resulting from conditions of poverty, as was also the case in England[325]. If the systematic fires started by farmers, peasants, hunters, and shepherds reflected the needs of rural populations inside reserves, they were also a sign of daily prevarication in royal reserves. After the Liberal Revolution, the same crimes were committed inside the National Woods, previously belonging to the Crown.

From the viewpoint of resources, reserves were kept by the Surveyor-General's Department. The latter also policed and to some extent limited the excessive use of those spaces. In that sense, in terms of wood reserves and mountain lands belonging to the Crown, the privilege of the maintenance of reserves was only replaced, by the figure of the Liberal State. Crown woods were fully preserved, and with the exception of royal parks, their management was transferred from an organisation dependent on the Crown to another one dependent on the State. The latter was the legitimate manager of a good valuable to the community. After the extinction of the Surveyor-General's Department, this resource had rapidly become dilapidated. Liberal parliamentarians soon acknowledged the need to stop this deterioration of the National Woods and create ways to regulate access to their use. This was in order to prevent the same crimes of banditry as previously fought by the Department.

Only in 1800, ten years after the establishment of the system that aimed at standardising the State's judicial machine, the Surveyor-General's Department was put partially under the supervision of territorial authorities. It continued to enjoy a special judicial status. In addition, from 1800 onwards, wood reserves went on enjoying judicial and administrative autonomy. Furthermore, because it was an autonomous organisation derived from the Crown and with the key role of guaranteeing the Crown's prerogatives, it created ideal conditions for the establishment of smuggling networks. The very owners of coercive means and legal guarantees and those responsible for enforcement further ensured this. The manipulation of notary registrars in reserves, together with mechanisms of coercion and easy transportation at loading quays by reserves, facilitated their activities. In most cases, these were practised with impunity.

At an institutional level, this independence from jurisdictional structures allowed the Crown, through the Surveyor-General's Department, to project its influence on the territory in a pervasive way. This was mingled with resistance from municipalities and landlords. Having the duty and exclusive right to lead wolf hunts all over the country, the Surveyor-General's Department had a territorial influence that clearly exceeded the one of royal reserves. Interfering in the jurisdictional areas and spheres of power of other Ancient Regime bodies, particularly those of municipalities, this generated numerous conflicts.

The autonomy of the Surveyor-General's Department in lands within royal reserves and the ramification of the kingdom's jurisdiction throughout the whole country gave it a unique power. This organisation was a force that competed with other Ancient Regime influences, namely municipalities and seigniorial power.

Surveyor-Generals of His Majesty's Woods and Forests
Brief chronology

D. Fernando José de Melo, 1777-1787

Successor to the House of Surveyor-Generals, he received his letter of office on May 27th 1777. "Noble Man of His Majesty's Chamber"[326], a post he occupied for ten years until his death, on January 29th 1787.

D. Francisco José Luís de Melo, 1787-1789

Did not receive a Surveyor-General's letter of office [327]. The son of D. Fernando José de Melo, he inherited his father's post and ran the Surveyor-General's Department for two years. He died of smallpox at the age of eighteen, on January 24th 1789, and left no successor[328].

D. Francisco José (de Melo) da Cunha Mendonça e Meneses, 1789-1806

Successor to his cousin D. Francisco José Luís de Melo, he received his office letter on February 16th 1789, "having the obligation of using it immediately after his name, the family name Melo, according to the institution of the house's eldest son, of which he will be the heir"[329].

Heir to the Lords of Valdigem, 1st Count of Castro Marim in 1802, and 1st Marquis of Olhão in 1808, Governor of Arms of Alentejo and the Algarve. He led the rebellion against the French in 1808, and was member of the Regency in the same year.

D. Pedro José de Melo da Cunha Mendonça e Meneses, 1806-1834

1806 – 1808: Surveyor-General.
1808 – 1812 Under Junot's government, he was Inspector General of Woods and Reserved Parks.
1808 – 1821: Surveyor-General in office.
1821 – 1823: The post of Surveyor-General is abolished. He kept the title of the Royal House.
1823 – 1834: He recovered the post of Surveyor-General.
1826 Appointed peer of the kingdom.
1833 President of the Municipality of Lisbon[330].

SOURCES AND BIBLIOGRAPHY

MANUSCRIPT SOURCES
Arquivo Histórico do Ministério do Equipamento, Planeamento e Ordenamento do Território / former Ministério das Obras Públicas (Historical Archive of the Planning, Equipment and Territorial Administration Office, former Public Works Office)

MONTARIA-MOR DO REINO, SERIES 1 to 40
Series of the documental nucleus of the MMR

1 – Correspondence Record Books – record of entries and summaries of correspondence, 1533-1833, with no kind of organisation.

2 – Correspondence Copy Books on transgressions, statements and other documents, 1777-1821 and 1724-1833.

3 – Personal record of the royal reserves of Salvaterra de Magos.

4 – Record of gamekeepers on horseback and farm servants, their weapons and documents concerning them.

5 – ABC of reserve posts.

6 – Record of expenses and revenues with reserve officers.

7 – Alphabetical index of Portuguese lands.

8 – Regulations, official documents and other documents regarding management – 1605 until the 19th century.

9 – Royal orders and warnings from the State Office of the Kingdom's Businesses, 1596-1721.

10 – Warnings from the State Office of the Kingdom's Businesses on petitions and pardons (connection with nucleus no. 2), 1738-1833.

11 – Royal orders, warnings of the State Office of the Kingdom and petitions regarding the Falconry of Salvaterra de Magos, 1756-1806.

12 – Edicts.

13 – Certificates of the issue of edicts, 1758-1810.

14 – List of employees and officers of the Surveyor-General's Department (connection with nucleus no. 4), 1732-1818.

15 – Job requests informed by council chambers and certificates for the payment of wages to reserve officers, 1770-1833.

16 – Correspondence of employees, and petitions (reserve officers' reports, correspondence on resource management and some crime processes), 1583-1833.

17 – Processes (licenses for: cut down of timber, sticks and tree branches and foliage; gathering of firewood, undergrowth and stumps; ground clearances by fire, creation of coal-production factories and pasture usage), 1722-1883.

18 – Lists of petitions originating in Royal Dispatches (Nucleus no. 2 – record of transgressions – contains part of these petitions and Surveyor-Generals' answers), 1828-1833.

19 – Hunts – in reserved areas, 1777-1786.

20 – Hunts at the reserve of Almeirim, 1780-1786.

21 – Hunts at the reserve of Benavente.

22 – Hunts at the reserve of Coruche, 1780-1786.

23 – Hunts at the reserve of Muja.

24 – Hunts at the reserve of Pinheiro.

25 – Hunts at the reserve of Salvaterra.

26 – Hunts at the reserve of Samora and Belmonte.

27 – Hunts at the reserve of Santarém, 1775-1789.

   – Regulations of 1775.

   – Map of the reserves of Santarém, 1777.

   – Correspondence on stubbling up, ground clearing by fire and conversion of land for agriculture at the reserves of Almeirim and Santarém between 1775 and 1777.

28 – List of beaters, 1770-1786.

29 – List of wild boar and deer hunting parties at reserves.

30 – Documents on hunting licenses, 1763-1828.

31 – Documents regarding the inspection of woods and parks of the kingdom and Report of Purveyors', Districts' and Magistrates' Offices of 1808.

32 – Lists of employees to be paid.

33 – Fee-farm letters of the rentier contarct with Rolim, 1786.

34 – Records made by the magistrate Luís Vieira, 1617.

35 – Documents received and sent by the reserve judge and magistrate António de Freitas Branco, 1683-1710.

36 – Embargoes on employees' appointments.

37 – Testimonies and decisive instruments.

38 – Inquiries, exemption of guilt and crime processes (contains, by chronological order, documents from 1702 until 1817. These processes, amounting to 40, are divided in three packets, each containing precise chronological limits. The first one goes from 1702 to 1754 and contains 12 processes; the second one goes from 1758 to 1778 and contains 16 processes, 6 of which concern the years of 1777 and 1778; the third and last one goes from 1779-1817 and contains 12 processes, 1702-1817.

39 – Verdict of cartulary, measuring and boundary line definition, 1761 (farm at Rio de Milho).

40 – Civil verdicts of justification.

ARQUIVO NACIONAL DA TORRE DO TOMBO (NATIONAL ARCHIVE OF THE TORRE DO TOMBO)

Arquivo da Casa Real (Archive of the Royal House) – Index no. 512.

Ministério do Reino (Kingdom's Office), packet 281.

- Inquiry and crime process started in 1815 on the reserve judge of Sintra who had managed the lands of the House of the Queens as though they belonged to him.
- Correspondence exchanged between the Surveyor-General, Count of Castro Marim and D. João VI, based in Brazil, 1810-1812.

Registo Geral das Mercês (General Record of Mercês)

ARQUIVO MUNICIPAL DE BENAVENTE (MUNICIPAL ARCHIVE OF BENAVENTE)

- Crime processes and accusation documents against poachers.

BIBLIOTECA DA AJUDA (LIBRARY OF AJUDA)

- Regulations of the reserve of Lisbon, 44 VIII 61 (no. 1-a-b).
- Regulations of the reserve of Sintra, 44 XIII 61 (no. 2-a-i).
- Regulations of the reserve of Benavente, 44 XVIII 61 (no. 3-a-d).
- Regulations of the reserve of Muja, 44 XIII 61 (no. 5 a and b).
- Regulations of the reserve of Óbidos, 44 XIII (no. 5 and no. 7).
- Regulations of the reserve of Salvaterra de Magos, 44 XIII (no. 9 d).
- Regulations of the reserve of Coruche, 44 XIII 61 (no. 10).
- Regulations of the reserve of Santarém, 44 VIII.

BIBLIOTECA NACIONAL DE LISBOA – SECÇÃO DE RESERVADOS (NATIONAL LIBRARY – RESERVED SECTION)

Aviso de caçadores e caça. Ordenado por el Doctor Nuñez de Avenduño: Letrado de don Yñigo Lopez de Mendonça tercero deste nombre, Duque del Infantado con nuevas Adiciones, 1593 – Res. 758 / 2.

Descripção das coutadas e casas de campo dos príncipes de Portugal in Miscelânea, Res. – cod. 10768, fol. 215 v.º-217, no date.

Monteiro-Mor – Res. – Box 27, no. 105.

Regimento da Coutada de Muja – Res. – cod. 11796, fol. 356.

Regimento da Coutada de Salvaterra de Magos – Res. – cod. 7667.

Regimento dos Monteiros-Mores (1751) – Res. – Box 31, no. 4.

PUBLISHED SOURCES
Codes and Legislation

Albuquerque, António Tavares de – *Índice Alfabético e Remissivo dos Trabalhos Parlamentares das Cortes Gerais e Extraordinárias da Nação Portuguesa 1821-1823.*

Branco, Alípio Freire de Figueiredo Abreu Castelo – *Repertório ou Índice Geral Alfabético e Remissivo de toda a legislação publicada desde Julho de 1840 até Dezembro de 1847*, Lisbon, Imprensa Nacional, 1847.

Branco, Alípio Freire de Figueiredo Abreu Castelo – *Repertório Alfabético da Legislação publicada desde Julho de 1848 até Dezembro de 1867*, Lisbon, Imprensa Nacional, 1868.

Carvalho, Porfírio Hemétrio Homem de – *Primeiras Linhas do Direito Agrário Deste Reino*, Lisbon, Impressão Régia, 1815.

Código Administrativo anotado, Lisbon, Imprensa Nacional, 1852.

Código Civil Português, aprovado por carta de lei de 1 de Julho de 1867, Lisbon, Imprensa Nacional, 1868.

Código Penal, Lisbon, Imprensa Nacional, 1852.

Ordenações Afonsinas – vols. I-V, Lisbon, Fundação Calouste Gulbenkian, 1984.

Ordenações Filipinas – vols. I-V, Lisbon, Fundação Calouste Gulbenkian, 1985.

Ordenações Manuelinas – vols. I-V, Lisbon, Fundação Calouste Gulbenkian, 1984.

Regimento para a Guarda Mór dos Pinhais de Leiria, e Superintendente da Fábrica de Madeira da Marinha, e seus Officiais, no qual se dá a forma para o bem do governo, e arrecadação da Fazenda Real 1751, Lisbon, Imprensa Régia.

Regulamento da Administração das Matas, 1824, Lisbon, Impressão Régia, 1824.

Silva, António Delgado da – *Colecção de Legislação Portuguesa desde a Última Compilação das Ordenações*, 6 vols., Lisbon, 1825-1830.

Silva, José Justino de Andrade e – *Colecção cronológica compilada e anotada por José Justino de Andrade e Silva*, Lisbon, 1854-1859.

Silva, José Justino de Andrade e – *Repertório Geral ou Índice Alfabético e Remissivo da Legislação Portuguesa Publicada desde o ano de 1815 até ao ano de 1849, em Continuação ao de Fernandes Tomás*, 2nd ed., increased with the legislation of 1850, Lisbon, author's printing, 1850, 2 vols.

Tomás, Manuel Fernandes – *Repertório Geral ou Índice Alfabético das Leis Extravagantes do Reino de Portugal, 1815-1819*, 2nd ed., corrected and increased, Coimbra, Imprensa da Universidade, 1843.

TREATIES

Argote de Molina, Gonzalo – *Discurso Sobre La Monteria, 1582 (Con otro Discurso Y Notas del Exmo. Señor D. José Gutierrez de La Vega* – single volume, Madrid, 1882.

D. Duarte – *Leal Conselheiro o qual fez D. Eduarte Rei de Portugal e do Algarve e senhor de Ceuta*, Porto, Lello & Irmãos Editores, 1981.

D. Duarte – *Livro da Ensinança de Bem Cavalgar a Toda a Sela que fez El-Rey Dom Eduarte de Portugal e do Algarve e senhor de Ceuta – Col. Tesouros da Literatura e da História*, Porto, Lello & Irmãos Editores, 1981.

D. Duarte – *Livro da Montaria Composto Pelo Senhor Rey Dom João de Portugal, e dos Algarves, e senhor de Ceuta – Col. Tesouros da Literatura e da História*, Porto, Lello & Irmãos Editores, 1981.

Farriéres, Henri de – *Le Libre de La Chasse du roy Modus*, Paris, Émile Noutry Éditeur, Librairie Cynégétique, 1931.

Faria, Manuel Severim de – *Discursos Vários Políticos, por Manuel Severim de Faria, novamente reimpressos e corrigidos segundo a edição de 1624*, Lisbon, Imprensa Régia, 1805.

Gama, L. A. Ludovice da – *Resumo da caça Ordinária, Poesia e Siência do Caçador Rústico*, Lisbon, Typografia da Gazeta de Portugal, 1866.

Martínez de Espinar, Alonso – *Arte de Ballesteria Y Montería*, Madrid, 1944.

Marcos, Juan – *Origen Y Dignidad de la Caza (1634)*, Madrid, 1966.

Oliveira, Luís da Silva Pereira – *Privilégios da Nobreza e Fidalguia de Portugal*, Lisbon, 1806.

Perrin, Beneton de – *Eloge Historique de la Chasse*, Paris, Morel le jeune, grand'salle du Palais au grand Cyrus; Gonuchon, rue de la Huchette, Briasson, rue de S. Jacques, à la Science, Guillaume, quay des Augustins à Saint Charles, 1824 (1st edition 1734).

GENERAL SOURCES

Aça, Zacarias de – *Almanach-Manual dos Caçadores*, Lisbon, Livraria de Cruz C.ª Editores, 1883.

Aça, Zacarias de – *Lisboa Moderna*, Lisbon, Livraria Editora Viúva Tavares Cardoso, 1907.

Almeida, Fialho de – *Estâncias de Arte e Saudade – Obras Completas*, Lisbon, Círculo de Leitores, no date.

Amaral, Joaquim Monteiro De Albuquerque e – *Allegações juridicas por Parte da Coroa sobre os Bens que no distrito de Pancas Possuira o Senhor D. Fernando, Duque de Bragança, e nos quais se Achavam Intrusos os Denominados Senhores de Pancas, Precedidas do Libello e Terminadas com o Auto de Exame sobre a Falsidade Praticada em hum Documento Junto aos Autos e com o Termo de Desistência, que do Mesmo se Fez*, Lisbon, Impressão Régia, 1805.

Barbosa, Domingos Caldas – *Descripção da grandiosa Quinta dos Senhore de Bellas, e noticia do seu Melhoramento Offerecida à Ilustrissima, e Excellentissima Senhora D. Maria Rita de Castelo Branco Correia e Cunha, Condeça de Pombeiro, e Senhora de Bellas*, Lisbon, Typographia Regia, 1799.

Barreiros, Montufar – *Caça*, Lisbon, A Literal Oficina Typográphica, 1900.

Coutinho, Rodrigo de Souza – *Textos Políticos Económicos e Financeiros 1783-1811*, Vol. II, Lisbon, Banco de Portugal, 1993.

Daun, Joseph S. de Saldanha Oliveira – *Memoria Historica sobre A Origem, Progresso, e Consequencias da Famoza Cauza da Denuncia de Pancas; que no Juizo da regia Corôa de Portugal, Ofereceu a Viuva D. Maria Balbina de Souza Coutinho contra os Actuais Senhores de Pancas D. Maria Leonor Manuel de Vilhena Costa Freire, e Seu Marido*, London, H. Bryer Street, Blackfriars, 1811.

Barreto, José Trazimundo Mascarenhas – *Memórias do Marquês de Fronteira e Alorna*, vols. I-IV, Lisbon, Imprensa Nacional Casa da Moeda, 1986 (facsimile of the edition of Coimbra, Imprensa da Universidade, 1928).

Delgado, Joaquim Filipe Nery da Encarnação; Ribeiro, Carlos – *Relatório Ácerca da Arborização Geral do Paiz*, Lisbon, Typografia da Academia Real de Ciências, 1868.

Diário das Cortes Gerais e Extraordinárias da Nação Portuguesa, Lisbon, Imprensa Nacional, 1821-1823.

Gazeta de Lisboa, Imprensa Régia, 1777-1820.

Junta Geral do Distrito de Lisboa – *Relatório Regulamentar sobre o exercício da caça*, 1879.

Leão, Miguel Lopes de – *Analyse Juridico-Critica da Alegação Historico-Juridica, que na Causa de Denuncia de Bens de Pancas compoz o Doutor Miguel Lopes de Leão Advogado da Casa da Suplicação. Oferecida a Illustrissima e Excellentissima D. Maria Balbina de Sousa Coutinho*, Lisbon, Impressão Régia, 1804.

Leão, Miguel Lopes de – *Segunda Alegação Historico-Juridica em Resposta Demonstrativa com originais Documentos dos Erros de Facto, e de Direito das Allegações Adversas, e Notas Anonimas; e com Huma Dissertação Convincente da Fabulosa Falsidade que vã, e inutilmente se introduziu na Causa da Denuncia do Morgado de Pancas, contra a Excellentissima D. Maria Balbina de Sousa Coutinho, a favor da Excellentissima D. Maria Leonor Carolina da Conceição Manoel de Vilhena e seu Marido José Sebastião de Saldanha, e Oliveira, no Juizo da Regia Coroa*, Lisbon, Officina de António Rodrigues Galhardo, 1805.

Leão, Miguel Lopes de – *Impugnação Compendiosa aos Dilatados, Sofisticos, e Falsos Embargos que por parte da D. Maria Balbina de Sousa Coutinho Attentadamente se Formarão A' Justissima Sentença contra ella proferida no Juizo da Coroa, sobre a Denuncia da Fazenda e Morgado de Pancas, em Sustentação, e Defesa da Mesma Respeitabilissima Sentença a Favor da Excellentissima D. Maria Leonor Carolina da Conceição Manoel de Vilhena e seu Marido Excellentissimo José Sebastião de Saldanha Oliveira e Daun*, Officina de Simão Thadeu Ferreira, 1806.

Memórias Económicas da Academia Real das Ciências de Lisboa, 1789-1815, vols. I-V, Lisbon, Banco de Portugal, 1991.

Neves, José Acúrsio das – *Obras Completas de José Acúrsio das Neves*, vols. 1 and 2, Porto, Afrontamento, no date.

Observações Gerais sobre um novo plano de Administração Geral das Matas do Reino seguidas do módico prático da sua Criação, cultura, e augmento; E de tirar toda a conveniente vantagem d'estas preciosas propriedades do estado, por um empregado na Administração Geral das Matas, Imprensa de Cândido António da Silva Carvalho, at the end of the Calçada do Garcia no. 42, Lisbon, 1834.

Pinto, Albano da Silveira – *Resenha das Famílias e Titulares e Grandes de Portugal*, Lisbon, vol. II, 1883-1890.

Vandelli, Domingos – *Aritmética Política e Finanças 1770-1804*, Lisbon, Banco de Portugal, 1994.

SPECIFIC BIBLIOGRAPHY

Almeida, Jayme Duarte – "A caça em Portugal Através dos Tempos" in *A Caça em Portugal*, coord. Carlos Eurico da Costa, Lisbon, 2 vols., 4th edition, Editorial Estampa, 1994 (1st edition 1963).

Beinart, William – "The Night of the Jackal: Sheep, Pastures and Predators in the Cape" in *Past & Present*, no. 158 (1998).

Boletim da Direcção-Geral de Agricultura, 8th year, no. 3, 1st part, Lisbon, Imprensa Nacional, 1908.

Bouza, Fernando; Senos, Nuno; Hespanha, António et Cardim, Pedro (eds.) – *Cartas para duas infantas meninas: Portugal na correspondência de D. Filipe I para suas filhas, 1581-1583*, Lisboa, Publicações D. Quixote, 1998.

Broad, John – "Wigs, Deer-stealers and the Origins of the Black Act" in *Past & Present*, no. 119 (May 1988), pp. 56-72.

Cardim, Pedro – "Centralização política e estado na Recente Historiografia sobre o Portugal de Antigo regime"in *Nação e Defesa,* Nº87, Outono 98, 2ª série, Instituto de Defesa nacional, Lisboa, 1998, pp 129-158

Cardim, Pedro – " Religião e ordem social em Torno dos Fundamentos Católicos do Sistema Político do Antigo regime", in *separata da Revista de História das Ideias*, vol 22, Faculdade de Letras, Coimbra, 2001, pp 133-174

Conde de Ybes – *Veinte Años de Caza Maior* – prologue by Ortega Y Gasset, Espasa-calpse, S.A., Madrid, 1943.

Correia, Joaquim Manuel da Silva; Guedes, Natália Brito Correia – *O Paço Real e Salvaterra de Magos: a Corte, a Ópera, a Falcoaria*, Lisbon, Livros Horizonte, 1989.

Correia, José Eduardo Horta – *Liberalismo e Catolicismo: O Problema Congreganista (1820-1823)*, Coimbra, Universidade de Coimbra, 1974.

Corvol, Andrée, *Histoire de la Chasse*, Paris, 2010.

Corvol, Andrée *L'Homme aux Bois. Histoire des Relations del l'Homme et de la Forêt XVIIe-XXe Siècle,* Paris, 1987.

Costa, Carlos Eurico da (dir.) – *A Caça em Portugal*, 2 vols., 4th edition, Lisbon, Editorial Estampa, 1994.

Costa, Maria Leonor Freire – *Naus e Galeões na Ribeira de Lisboa*, Cascais, Patrimónia, 1997.

Costa, Mário Alberto Nunes da – "A Montaria-Mor do Reino" in *Revista Portuguesa de História*, vol. XI (1996).

Curto, Diogo Ramada, *A cultura Política em Portugal (1578-1642). Comportamentos, Ritos e Negócios*, Tese de Doutoramento em Sociologia Histórica aprsentada à Faculdade de Ciências Sociais e Humanas da Universidade Nova de Lisboa, Lisboa, 1994.

Curto, Diogo Ramada – "Conclusões: Nobreza Manuelina e seus descendentes" in *D. Álvaro da Costa e a Sua Descendência, séculos XV-XVII: Poder, Arte e Devoção*, C oord. Maria Lurdes Rosa, CIEM – Instituto de Estudos Medievais, CHAM – Centro de Esttudos de Além-Mar, Caminhos Romanos, Lisboa, 2013, pp. 343-359, 351-352

Devy-Vareta, Nicole – *A Floresta no Espaço e no Tempo em Portugal – A Arborização da Serra da Cabreira (1919-1975)*, Porto, Faculdade de Letras da Universidade do Porto, 1993.

Devy-Vareta, Nicole – "Para uma Geografia Histórica da Floresta Portuguesa: As Matas Medievais e a 'Coutada Velha' do Rei" in *Revista da Faculdade de Letras – Geografia*, 1st series, vol. I (1985), pp. 47-67.

Devy-Vareta, Nicole – "Para uma Geografia Histórica da Floresta Portuguesa: do Declínio das Matas Medievais à Política Florestal do Renascimento (séc. XV e XVI)" in *Revista da Faculdade de Letras – Geografia*, 1st series, vol. I (1986), pp. 5-37.

Freeman, Michael – "Plebs or Predators? Deer-stealing in Whichwood Forest, Oxfordshire in the eighteenth and nineteenth centuries" in *Social History*, vol. 21, no. 1 (January).

Grassby, Richard – "The decline of Falconry in Early Modern England" in *Past & Present*, no. 157 (1997).

Labrador Arroyo, Felix – *La casa Real en Portugal(1580.1621)*, Madrid, Ediciones Polifemo, 2009.

Liddiard, Robert,(edit by), The Medieval Park, New Perspectives, Windgather Press, 2007.

Lopez Ontiveros, Antonio – "Algunos Aspectos de la Evolución de La Caza en España" in *Agricultura y Sociedad*, no. 58 (Enero-Marzo 1991), pp.47-51.

Lopez Ontiveros, Antonio – "Importancia de la geografia cinegética en el contexto de la geografia agrária española" in A. Gil Olcina e A. Morales Gil – *Medio siglo de los cambios agrarios en España* , Alicante, Instituto de Cultura Juan Gil Albert, no. 58, Enero-Marzo, 1991, pp.191-216.

Maltez, José Adelino – "O Estado e as Instituições" in *Nova História de Portugal, Direcção de Joel Serrão e A. H. De Oliveira Marques, Portugal do Renascimento à Crise Dinástica*, Coord, João José Alves Dias, Editorial Presença, 1998, pp. 337-412.

Melo, Cristina Joanaz de – *Coutadas reais: privilégio, poder, gestão e conflito (1777-1824)*, Lisboa, Montepio Geral, 2001.

Melo, Cristina Joanaz de – "Diana's torments: forests and hunting as a tool for social and political control in the Modern Age" in 'Working & Walking in the Footsteps of Ghosts: Part 2 - The History of Management', ISBN reference - 978-1-904098-54-6 Black & White version due to be published 2016

Monteiro Nuno e Oliveira, César de (dir.) – *História dos Municípios e do Poder Local (dos finais da Idade Média à união europeia)*, Lisbon, Círculo de Leitores, 1996.

Nahon, Guillaume – *La Révolution et la Chasse*, Union Nationale des Fédérations Départementeles.

Neves, C. M. Baeta – "Dos Monteiros-Mores aos Engenheiros Silvicultores" in *Anais do Instituto Superior de Agronomia*, vol. XXVIII (1965).

Neves, C. M. Baeta – *História Florestal, Aquícola e Cinegética*, 6 vols., Lisbon, Ministério da Agricultura e Pescas – Direcção-Geral das Florestas, 1980-1991.

Paiva, José Pedro Paiva – "Um corpo entre outros corpos sociais: o clero" In *Revista de História das Ideias*, vol 33, 2012, pp165-182.

Pereira, João Cordeiro – "A estrutura Social e o Seu Devir" in *Nova História de Portugal, Direcção de Joel Serrão e A. H. De Oliveira Marques, Portugal do Renascimento à Crise Dinástica*, Coord, João José Alves Dias, Editorial Presença, 1998, pp. 277-336.

Pérez Vicente, Isabel – "Legislación Cinegética en España: Evolución Y Actualidad" in *Agricultura y Sociedad*, no. 58 (Enero-Marzo 1991), pp.173-213.

Radich, Maria Carlos – *Agronomia no Portugal Oitocentista: uma Discreta Desordem*, Oeiras, Celta Editora, 1996.

Ribeiro, Margarida – *Coruche, Estudo Histórico*, 1959.

Riley, Carlos Guilherme – *Sobre a Caça Medieval*, Coimbra, 1988.

Rivera Mateos, Manuel – "Caza y Agricultura en Zonas de Montaña" in *Agricultura y Sociedad*, no. 58 (Enero-Marzo 1991), pp.113-145.

Rocha, Manuel Coelho da – *Instituições de Direito Civil Português*, Coimbra, 1907.

Rúbio Aragonés, Maria José – *La Caza y la Casa Real*, Badajoz, Ayuntamiento de Badajoz, 1996.

Saramago, Alfredo – *A Caça. Perspectiva Histórica e Receitas Tradicionais*, Colares, Colares Editora.

Salvadori, Phillipe – *La Chasse Sous l'Ancient Régime*, Paris, Fayard, 1996.

Silbert, Albert – *Le Problème Agraire Portugais au Temps des Premières Cortes Libérales*, Paris, Fondation Calouste Gulbenkian, 1985.

Silbert, Albert – *Le Portugal Méditérranéen à la Fin de l'Ancient Régime XVIII – Début du XIX Siècle*, 2nd edition, Lisbon, INIC, 3 vols.

Silva, Hugo Ribeiro da, *O Clero Catedralício Português e os Equilíbrios Sociais do Poder*, Lisboa, CEHR-Universidade Católica Portuguesa, 2013

Thompson, E. P. – *Wigs & Hunters*, London, Penguin, 1990.

Valente, Vasco Pulido – "O Povo em Armas: a Revolta Nacional de 1808-1809" in *Análise Social*, 2nd series, vol. XV (57) (1979), 1st, pp.7-48.

GENERAL BIBLIOGRAPHY

Cardoso, Óscar – *A Espingarda de Caça em Portugal: Grandes Marcas, Balística & Outras Artes*, Lisbon, Edições Inapa, 1996.

Carvalho, José Paulo Mirae de – *Uma Noção de Caça ao Javali*, 2nd edition, Évora, Typografia do Governo Civil, 1874.

Coelho, Maria Helena da C.; Magalhães, Joaquim Romero – *O Poder Concelhio: das Origens às Cortes Constituintes*, Coimbra, Centro de Estudos e Formação Autárquica, 1986.

Elias, Norbert – *A Sociedade de Corte*, Lisbon, Editorial Estampa, 1987.

Fernandes, Paulo Jorge – *As Faces de Proteu: Elites Urbanas e Poder Municipal em Lisboa de Finais do Século XVIII a 1851*, Lisbon, Câmara Municipal de Lisboa, 1999.

Fonseca, Helder Adegar – *O Alentejo no Século XIX. Economia e Atitudes Económias*, Lisbon, Imprensa Nacional, 1996.

Gaspar, Jorge – *A Área de Influência de Évora. Sistemas de Funções e Lugares Centrais*, Lisbon, CEG/INIC, 1972.

Herculano, Alexandre – *Opúsculos*, vols. I-VI, Lisbon, Editorial Presença, 1982.

Hespanha, António Manuel – *As Vésperas do Leviathan: Instituições e Poder Político*, Coimbra, Almedina, 1994.

Lains, Pedro – *A Economia Portuguesa no Séc. XIX,* Lisbon, Imprensa Nacional Casa da Moeda, 1994.

Justino, David – *O Atraso Económico Nacional: Portugal 1820-1913*, 2 vols., Lisbon, Vega.

Mattoso, José – *História de Portugal*, vols. III and IV, Lisbon, Círculo de Leitores, 1993.

Monteiro, Nuno Gonçalo – *O Crepúsculo dos Grandes Portugueses (1750-1832)*, Lisbon, Imprensa Nacional Casa da Moeda, 1998.

Monteiro, Nuno Gonçalo – "Os Concelhos e as Comunidades" in Mattoso, José, dir. and coord. – *História de Portugal*, Lisbon, Círculo de Leitores, 1993, vol. IV.

Monteiro, Nuno Gonçalo – "Poder Senhorial, Estatuto Nobiliárquico e Aristocracia" in Mattoso, José, dir. and coord. – *História de Portugal*, Lisbon, Círculo de Leitores, 1993, vol. IV.

Monteiro, Nuno Gonçalo – "Revolução Liberal e Regime Senhorial: a Questão dos Forais na Conjuntura Vintista" in *Revista Portuguesa de História*, XXIII, Coimbra (1987), pp. 143-182.

Neto, Maria Margarida Sobral – *A População de Mira e a Desamortização dos Baldios na Segunda Metade do Século XIX*, Coimbra, Faculdade de Letras – Instituto de História Económica e Social, 1982.

Oliveira, César de (dir.) – *História dos Municípios e do Poder Local*, Lisbon, Círculo de Leitores, 1996.

Ortega y Gasset, José – *La Caza Y los Toros*, 2nd edition, Madrid, Revista de Ocidente, 1968.

Pedro, António Mário – *Aspectos da Vida Quotidiana de D. João V*, Lisbon, graduation thesis in History, Universidade de Lisboa, Faculdade de Letras, 1966.

Pereira, Paulo (dir.) – *História da Arte Portuguesa*, vols. 1-3, Lisbon, Círculo de Leitores, 1995.

Peres, Damião (dir.) – *História de Portugal*, vols. VI-VII, Porto, Portucalense Editora, 1934.

Pimentel, José Cortez – *Arrábida: História de uma Região Privilegiada*, Lisbon, Edições Inapa, 1992.

Pereira, Míriam Halpern Pereira – *Livre Câmbio e Desenvolvimento Económico: Portugal na Segunda Metade do Séc. XIX*, Lisbon, Cosmos, 1971.

Pereira, Míriam Halpern Pereira – *Revolução, Finanças e Dependência Externa*, vol. 1, Lisbon, Sá da Costa, 1979.

Pijoan, J. – *História da Arte Universal*, vol. 6, Lisbon, Alfa, 1989.

Reis, Jaime – *O Atraso Económico em Perspectiva Histórica: Estudos Sobre a Economia Portuguesa na Segunda Metade do Século XIX (1850-1930)*, Lisbon, Imprensa Nacional Casa da Moeda, 1993.

Rosado, António Augusto Cascales – *Caça Grossa em Portugal, Apontamentos*, Oeiras, autor's edition, 1991.

Saboul, Albert – *Problèmes Paysans de la Révolution 1789-1848*, Paris, François Maspero, 1976 (1st edition 1960).

Silveira, Luís Nuno Espinha da – *Revolução Liberal e Propriedade. A Venda dos Bens Nacionais no Distrito de Évora (1834-1852)*, Lisbon, PhD thesis in History, Universidade Nova de Lisboa, FCSH, 1988.

Silveira, Luís Nuno Espinha da – *Território e Poder: nas Origens do Estado Contemporâneo em Portugal*, Patrimonia Historica, Cascais, 1997.

Tengarrinha, José – *Movimentos Populares Agrários em Portugal*, 2 vols., Mem-Martins, Publicações Europa-América, 1994.

Vasconcelos, Carolina Michaelis de – "Mestre Giraldo e os Seus Tratados de Alveitaria e Cetraria" in *Revista Lusitana*, vol. XIII, no. 3 (1910) and no. 4 (1911).

Vieira, José Neiva – "Falemos da Nossa História Florestal" in *Mediterrâneo*, no.7, Instituto Mediterrânico da Universidade Nova de Lisboa, 1995.

Viterbo, Fr. Joaquim de Santa Rosa de – *Elucidário das Palavras, Termos e Frases*, vol. II, Lisbon, Ed. Crítica, 1966.

Woronoff, Denis – *Révolution et Espaces Forestiers*, preface by Michel Vovelle, Groupe d'Histoire des Fôrets Françaises, Paris.

Zulaica, Joseba – *Caza, Símbolo y Eros*, Madrid, Ediciones Nerea, 1992.

ICONOGRAPHIC ANNEX

Picture 1 – Portal of Saint Hubert's chapel in Amboise, France. Photo by Margarida Guerra Machado, 1995.

Picture 2 – Chambord castle, 17th century. Photo by Cristina Joanaz, 1995.

Picture 3 – Brigantine, tile panel, 18th century. Seminary of Santarém. Photo by José António Victorino, 1998.

Picture 4 – Equipment for a falconry hunt, tile panel, 18th century. Seminary of Santarém. Photo by José António Victorino, 1998.

Picture 5 – Deer hunt with a slip-knot, tile panel, 18th century. Seminary of Santarém. Photo by José António Victorino, 1998.

Picture 6 – Deer hunt with a spear, tile panel, 18th century. Seminary of Santarém. Photo by José António Victorino, 1998.

Picture 7 – Wild boar hunt with a spear, tile panel, 18th century. Seminary of Santarém. Photo by José António Victorino, 1998.

Picture 8 – Preparing wild boar meat, tile panel, 18th century. Seminary of Santarém. Photo by José António Victorino, 1998.

Picture 9 – Chasing birds with a net, tile panel, 18th century. Seminary of Santarém. Photo by José António Victorino, 1998.

Picture 10 – Detail of the bird chase with a net, tile panel, 18th century. Seminary of Santarém. Photo by José António Victorino, 1998.

Picture 11 – Detail of the bird chase with a net, tile panel, 18th century. Seminary of Santarém. Photo by José António Victorino, 1998.

Picture 12 – Bird hunt with a firearm, tile panel, 18th century. Seminary of Santarém. Photo by José António Victorino, 1998.

Picture 13 – Rabit hunt with a stick, tile panel, 18th century. Seminary of Santarém. Photo by José António Victorino, 1998.

Picture 14 – Lion hunt (literature elements included), tile panel, 18th century. Seminary of Santarém. Photo by José António Victorino, 1998.

Picture 15 – Bear hunt (inclusion of Medieval literature subjects), tile panel, 18th century. Seminary of Santarém. Photo by José António Victorino, 1998.

[1] Monteiro Nuno e Oliveira, César de (dir.) – *História dos Municípios e do Poder Local (dos finais da Idade Média à união europeia)*, Lisbon, Círculo de Leitores, 1996.

[2] "Diana's torments: forests and hunting as a tool for social and political control in the Modern Age" in 'Working & Walking in the Footsteps of Ghosts: Part 2 - The History of Management', ISBN reference - 978-1-904098-54-6 Black & White version due to be published Decembre 2014

[3] Corvol, Andrée *L'Homme aux Bois. Histoire des Relations del l'Homme et de la Forêt XVIIe-XXe Siècle,* Paris, 1987.

[4] Corvol, Andrée, *Histoire de la Chasse,* Paris, 2010.

[5] The idea that the balance of powers at a local sphere and any attempt to deny consecrated local rights might have impacts of international proportions is borrowed from a different work of Hugo Silva. It deals with the connections of how local, namely ecclesial powers were deeply bonded with Imperial decision making; how the attempt to cut social bodies prerogatives, apparently at a local scale, could deeply collide with crowns interests in the context of the wars of religion in the 16th and 17th centuries; how the attempt to make Portuguese clergy pay a tribute to sustain the cost of Spanish wars against the Dutch and English in the Pacific and India, approved by Rome, wanted by the Spanish King but officially disapproved by the last, were determinant to launch the Aclamation War in Portugal, against the Spanish administration, in 1640. Silva, Hugo Ribeiro da, *O Clero Catedralício Português e os Equilíbrios Sociais do Poder*, Lisboa, CEHR-UCP, 2013

Regarding the centralization and organisation of bodies, look at Cardim, Pedro "Centralização política e estado na Recente Historiografia sobre o Portugal de Antigo regime"in *Nação e Defesa,* N°87, Outono 98, 2ª série, Instituto de Defesa nacional, Lisboa, 1998, pp 129-158; *Idem,* " Religião e ordem social em Torno dos Fundamentos Católicos do Sistema Político do Antigo regime", in *separata da Revista de História das Ideias*, vol 22, Faculdade de Letras, Coimbra, 2001, pp 133-174; Curto, Diogo Ramada, *A cultura Política em Portugal (1578-1642). Comportamentos, Ritos e Negócios*, Tese de Doutoramento em Sociologia Histórica aprsentada à Faculdade de Ciências Sociais e Humanas da Universidade Nova de Lisboa, Lisboa, 1994; *Idem* "Conclusões: Nobreza Manuelina e seus descendentes" in *D. Álvaro da Costa e a Sua Descendência, séculos XV-XVII: Poder, Arte e Devoção,* C oord. Maria Lurdes Rosa, CIEM – Instituto de Estudos Medievais, CHAM – Centro de Esttudos de Além-Mar, Caminhos Romanos, Lisboa, 2013, pp. 343-359, 351-352; Maltez, José Adelino, "O Estado e as Instituições" in *Nova História de Portugal, Direcção de Joel Serrão e A. H. De Oliveira Marques, Portugal do Renascimento à Crise Dinástica*, Coord, João José Alves Dias, Editorial Presença, 1998, pp. 337-412; Paiva, José Pedro Paiva "Um corpo entre outros corpos sociais: o clero" In *Revista de História das Ideias*, vol 33, 2012, pp165-182; Pereira, João Cordeiro , "A estrutura Social e o Seu Devir" in *Nova História de Portugal, Direcção de Joel Serrão e A. H. De Oliveira Marques, Portugal do Renascimento à Crise Dinástica*, Coord, João José Alves Dias, Editorial Presença, 1998, pp. 277-336;

[6] Lopez Ontiveros, Antonio – "Algunos Aspectos de la Evolución de la Caza en España" in *Agricultura y Sociedad*, no. 58, January-March, 1991, pp 173-213; Beinart, William – "The night of the jackal: sheep, pastures and predators in the Cape" in *Past & Present*, no. 158, Oxford, Oxford University Press, 1998; Freeman, Michael – "Plebs or predators? Deer-stealing in Whichwood Forest, Oxfordshire, in the eighteenth and nineteenth centuries" in *Social History*, vol. 21, no. 1, January ; Grassby, Richard – "The decline of falconry in early modern England" in *Past & Present*, no. 157, Oxford, Oxford University Press, 1997; Corvol, Andrée, *Histoire de la Chasse,* Paris, 2010

[7] Thompson, E. P. – *Whigs and Hunters*, London, Penguin, [1969]1990; James, N.D. G., *A History of English Forestry*, Basil Blackwell, [1981] 1990, Oxford; Rúbio Aragonés, Maria José – *La Caza y la Casa Real*, Badajoz, Ayuntamiento de Badajoz, 1996; Salvadori, Philipe – *La Chasse Sous l'Ancien Régime*, Fayard, 1996 ; Liddiard, Robert,(edit by), The Medieval Park, New Perspectives, Windgather Press, 2007.

[8] Corvol, Andrée, *Histoire de la Chasse,* Paris, 2010.

[9] Liddiard, Robert,(edit by), The Medieval Park, New Perspectives, Windgather Press, 2007.

[10] Riley, Carlos Guilherme – *Sobre a Caça Medieval*, Coimbra, 1988.

[11] Costa, Maria Leonor – *Naus e Galeões na Ribeira de Lisboa*, Cascais, Património, 1997.

[12] Neves, C. M. Baeta – *História Florestal, Aquícola e Cinegética*, 6 vols., Ministério da Agricultura e Pescas – Direcção-Geral das Florestas, Lisbon, 1980-1991.

[13] Bouza, Fernando; Senos, Nuno; Hespanha, António et Cardim, Pedro (eds.) – *Cartas para duas infantas meninas: Portugal na correspondência de D. Filipe I para suas filhas, 1581-1583*, Lisboa, Publicações D. Quixote, 1998

[14] Devy-Varetta, Nicole – "Para uma Geografia Histórica da Floresta Portuguesa: as Matas Medievais e a "Coutada Velha" do Rei" in Leaflet of the *Revista da Faculdade de Letras* – Geography, I series, vol. I,

Oporto, 1985, pp 47-67; "Para uma Geografia Histórica da Floresta Portuguesa: do Declínio das Matas Medievais à Política Florestal do Renascimento (séc. XV e XVI)" in Leaflet of the *Revista da Faculdade de Letras* – Geography, I series, vol. I, Oporto, 1986, pp 5-37.

[15]*Idem, A Floresta no Espaço e no Tempo em Portugal – A Arborização da Serra da Cabreira (1919-1975)*, Oporto, Faculdade de Letras of the University of Oporto, 1993.

[16] Hespanha, António Manuel – *As Vésperas do Leviathan: Instituições e Poder Político*, Coimbra, Livraria Almedina, 1994.

[17] Labrador Arroyo, Felix – *La casa Real en Portugal(1580.1621)*, Madrid, Ediciones Polifemo, 2009.

[18] Lopez Ontiveros, Antonio – "Algunos Aspectos de la Evolución de la Caza en España" in *Agricultura y Sociedad*, no. 58, January-March, 1991, pp 173-213;

[19] Rúbio Aragonés, Maria José – *La Caza y la Casa Real*, Badajoz, Ayuntamiento de Badajoz, 1996.

[20] Salvadori, Philipe – *La Chasse Sous l'Ancien Régime*, Fayard, 1996.

[21] Salvadori, Philipe, op. cit., author's translation.

[22] Rúbio Aragonés, Maria José, op. cit.

[23] Melo, Cristina Joanaz de, *Coutadas Reais Entre 1777-1824. Privilégio, Poder, Gestão e Conflito*, Lisboa, Montepio - Geral, 2000.

[24] Salvadori, op. cit.

[25] Almeida, Jayme Duarte – "A caça em Portugal através dos tempos" in *A Caça em Portugal*, 2 vols., Costa, Carlos Eurico da, dir. and co-ord., 4th edition, Lisbon, Editorial Estampa, 1994.

[26] Regulations of the Surveyor-General's Department of 1605.

[27] Information gathered mainly in MMR-2-Books 1 and 2; MMR-10; MMR-15; MMR-16; MMR-17; MMR-30; MMR-37; MMR-38.

[28] Riley, op. cit; D. João I – *Livro da Montaria Composto pelo Rey D. João de Portugal, e dos Algarves, e Senhor de Ceuta – Col. Tesouros da Literatura e da História*, Porto, Lello & Irmãos-Editores, 1981.

[29] Between 1788 and 1792, the Marquis of Marialva presented a petition to the Surveyor-General's Department (MMR-16-1790-1792) to enlarge the reserve area of Cantanhede. The document sent by the Marquis of Marialva is not dated. However, the analysis of the nucleus MMR-14, roll of the servers of the Surveyor-General's Department, allowed us to understand that the registrar who signed this register worked for the Department during this period. On the other hand, until this time the woods required by the Marquis of Marialva belonged to the Crown and were enrolled in the Regulations of 1605.

[30] Caetano, Marcelo – *História do Direito Português 1140-1495*, 2nd edition, Lisbon, 1985; *Código de Caça*, Notes from José Manso Preto, Atlântida Editora, 1967.

[31]*Idem.*

[32] BNL Reservados – *Regimento da Coutada de Muja* – cod. 1796, fol. 356.

[33] In its original version, the text referred the "link between movable resources and landed property", which does not correspond to German law. I thank Eng. João Bugalho for calling my attention to this aspect.

[34] MMR-17-1777 – 18.08.1777 – Licence granted to António Correia de Sousa, coal dealer in Lisbon, to cut and reduce to coal the pieces of wood bought in the game reserves of Santarém; 26.02.1787 – Licence granted to D. Luiza Ignácia de Melo to buy 6 pieces of wood to a farmer who owns a pinewood located "on the edge of the reserve" of Alcácer; 25.04.1787 – Licence granted to Luís Francisco to buy the felling of trees in an allotment of uncultivated trees in the reserve of Coruche, "away from hunting bushes"; 06.07.1790 – Licence granted to João Pereira da Silva to make coal from the woods bought to the Marquis of Tancos in Vale de Gatos, the reserve of Coruche.

[35] MMR-16 – 1778-02.06.1778 – Letter sent by Setúbal's royal administrator and tax collector to the Surveyor-General.

[36]*Idem.*

[37] Both Pera and Comporta are located in the Setúbal peninsula.

[38] MMR-16 – 1778, 17.08.1778 – Letter sent by the royal magistrate of Setúbal to the Surveyor-General presenting the result of the investigation.

[39] Silbert, Albert, op. cit. – Petitions sent to the courts of Palmela, Canha and Montemor-o-Novo (petition no. 88b, p. 101), and Cantanhede (petition no. 15a, p. 114).

[40] Almeida, Jayme Duarte – "A caça em Portugal através dos tempos" in *A Caça em Portugal*, 2 vols., Costa, Carlos Eurico da, dir. and co-ord., 4th edition, Lisbon, Editorial Estampa, 1994; The regulation of cork trees, as well as hunting laws, is integrated in the Ordinances of D. Filipe II, in Books I and V.

[41] Ord. Book I. Tit. §§ 25 and 26.

[42] Ord. Book I. Tit. 58 § 15.

[43] Ord. Book V. Tit. 75.

[44] Ordinances of D. Filipe II, Book 5, Tit. 75.

⁴⁵Ord. Book 5. Tit. 77.
⁴⁶Carvalho, Porfírio Hemétrio Homem de – *Primeiras Linhas do Direito Agrário deste Reino*, Lisbon, royal imprint, 1815.
⁴⁷Ordinances of D. Filipe II, Book 5, Tit. 86.
⁴⁸Decree from February 1st 1758.
⁴⁹Letter from October 12th 1612.
⁵⁰Decree from February 23rd 1624.
⁵¹Decree from July 1st 1776.
⁵²Edict from February 28th 1781.
⁵³Decree from July 1st 1776.
⁵⁴Ord. Book 2. Tit. 49, § 7.
⁵⁵Edict from February 23rd 1624.
⁵⁶Ord. Book 5. Tit. 88.
⁵⁷Ord. Book 5. Tit. 88, § 2.
⁵⁸Edict from July 1st 1776; Carvalho, Porfírio Hemérito Homem de, op. cit.; MMR-12 – Edict from February 28th 1781.
⁵⁹Decree from July 1st 1776.
⁶⁰MMR-12 – Edict from February 28th 1781.
⁶¹Neves, José Acúrsio das Neves – *História Geral das Invasões dos Franceses em Portugal e da Restauração deste Reino*, complete works of José Acúrsio das Neves, introd. by António Almodôvar and Armando de Castro, vol. I, tomes I and II, Lisbon, Edições Afrontamento.
⁶²*Regimmento dos Monteiros Mores dos Lobos e mais bichos das comarcas do Reyno* (09-08-1549).
⁶³*Idem.*
⁶⁴*Idem.*
⁶⁵*Idem.*
⁶⁶Regulations of the Surveyor-General's Department of 1605; Hespanha, António Manuel, op. cit.; Devy-Varetta, Nicole, *A Floresta no Espaço e no Tempo em Portugal – A Arborização da Serra da Cabreira (1919-1975)*; Costa, Mário Alberto Nunes da – "The Surveyor-General's Department", in Leaflet of the *Revista Portuguesa de História*, vol. XI, 1966.
⁶⁷This map was drawn from the description in the Regulations of 1605, the information in the MMR archive and the Regulations of 1800. As the territorial divisions and the toponymy changed, the map is an approach to the areas included in royal reserves by the time indicated in those dates. The reserve of Vila Viçosa was excluded because it belonged to the House of Bragança and was therefore not managed by the Surveyor-General's Department.
⁶⁸This map was drawn from the description in the Regulations of 1605, the information in the MMR archive and the Regulations of 1800. As the territorial divisions and the toponymy changed, the map is an approach to the areas included in royal reserves by the time indicated in those dates. The reserve of Vila Viçosa was excluded because it belonged to the House of Bragança and was therefore not managed by the Surveyor-General's Department.
⁶⁹*Gazeta de Lisboa*, 1778-1790.
⁷⁰Costa, Leonor, op. cit.
⁷¹Idem; Regulations of the Leiria Pinewoods of 1751.
⁷²The concept of function (economic and political) is dealt with by Riley, op. cit.
⁷³Costa, Mário Alberto Nunes da, op. cit.; Almeida, Jayme Duarte de, op. cit.; Hespanha, António Manuel, op. cit.; Vieira, José Neiva, "Falemos da Nossa História Florestal" in *Mediterrâneo*, no. 7, Universidade Nova de Lisboa; Devy-Varetta, Nicole, op. cit.
⁷⁴Almeida, Jayme Duarte de, op. cit.; Costa, Mário Alberto Nunes da, op. cit.
⁷⁵MMR-15 – Between 1770 and 1833, this nucleus contains numerous certificates, petitions and payment receipts of the reserves' officers' wages, made every six months, in cash, cereals and forest resources.
⁷⁶Regulations of the Surveyor-General's Department of 1605, § 36: "immediately declaring the place where to cut down the referred wood, and thus where to take the dried wood from, this place being the one that does not hurt game species".
ᴬᴺ Royal estates that support all princes except the first-born.
⁷⁷MMR-16-1778 – 31.07.1778.
⁷⁸MMR-2-Book 1 – 26.09.1778 – Letter sent by the Surveyor-General to the chief gamekeeper of Alcácer confirming that D. Joana had no licence to cut down any of the pine trees in the reserve; MMR-17-1790 – 21.05.1790 – Licence granted to D. Maria Ana Josefa Xavier de Lima allowing her to transform old trees into coal in her property of Monte dos Condes, in the limits of Benavente, under the justification that she "cannot make it without a licence".

[79] MMR-2-Book 1 – 22.09.1779 – Letter from the reserve judge of Muja to the Surveyor-General.
[80] MMR-2-Book 1 – 02.12.1782 – Letter sent by the Surveyor-General to the Duke of Cadaval.
[81] Regulations of the Surveyor-General's Department of 1605, § 26.
[82] Idem, § 28.
[83] MMR-2-Book 1 – 05.1787.
[84] Regulations, Book 5. Tit. 88, § 5.
[85] MMR, nos. 8, 9, 10, 12, 13, 38.
[86] Pedro, António Mário – *Aspectos na Vida Quotidiana de D. João V*, History degree thesis – Faculdade de Letras da Universidade de Lisboa, Lisbon, 1966.
[87] *Gazeta de Lisboa*, 1705-1750.
[88] MMR-12 – Edict of February 28th 1781.
[89] Thompson, E. P., op. cit.
[90] *Idem.*
[91] MMR-38-1778 – Official inquiry process of the Arrábida reserve regarding the inclusion of the estates of the House of Aveiro in the Crown's properties; Pimentel, José Cortez, *Arrábida, História de uma Região Privilegiada*, 1st edition, Edições Inapa, Lisbon, 1992.
[92] *Idem.*
[93] MMR-19 to 23 corresponds to the nuclei of the watches kept in royal reserves; MMR-20 (Almeirim); MMR-21 (Benavente); MMR-22 (Coruche); MMR-23 (Muja); MMR-24 (Pinheiro); MMR-25 (Salvaterra); MMR-26 (Samora and Belmonte); MMR-27 (Santarém).
[94] MMR-27. The 1775 map of the Arquivo Histórico Ultramarino (overseas historical archive) was published in Correia, Joaquim Manuel da Silva; Guedes, Natália Brito Correia – *Paço Real de Salvaterra de Magos: a Corte, a Ópera, a Falcoaria* – Lisbon, Livros Horizonte, 1989. In this work, the option made was to present the 1777 reproduction of the map of the game reserves of Santarém, from the Arquivo Histórico do MOP/Ministério do Equipamento, Planeamento e Ordenamento do Território.
[95] MMR-38-1778 – Inquiry process against Manuel Rodrigues, gamekeeper of Coruche.
[96] MMR-16-1777 – 22.07.1777 – Letter from the judge of the reserve of Santarém to the Surveyor-General.
[97] MMR-2-Book 1 – 21.8.1777 – Order to the judge of the reserve of Santarém. The Surveyor-General confirms the order to set free in Benavente two prisoners who had already been considered innocent by Pina Manique.
[98] MMR-16-1777 – 20.7.1777 – Order to the judge Pina Manique to proceed to the inquiry of fires in Benavente and Samora, and help the judges of Benavente and Santarém in that matter.
[99] MMR-16-1778 – 05.08.1778.
[100] MMR-38 – 06.01.1779 – Document of inquiry of special committee.
[101] *Idem.*
[102] *Idem.*
[103] MMR-16-1777, 12.07.1777 – Letter from the judge of Salvaterra to the Surveyor-General.
[104] MMR-16-1779 – 30.09.1779 – Bribe charge made by the reserve judge of Óbidos against the Surveyor-General of that same reserve; MMR-2-Book 1 – 24.07.86 – Arrest warrant for the reserve judge and gamekeeper of the reserve of Óbidos, sent to the judge of that village because of his guilt in "calling up to himself the office of that same judge, office which, as is told, is in power of someone whom without permission that judge appointed as registrar of the mentioned reserve".
[105] MMR-2-Book 1 – 08.08.1976.
[106] *Idem.*
[107] MMR-2-Book 1 – 8.08.1976.
[108] *Idem.*
[109] *Idem.*
[110] *Idem.*
[111] *Idem.*
[112] *Idem.*
[113] *Idem.*
[114] *Idem.*
[115] *Idem.*
[116] *Idem.*
[117] *Idem.*
[118] *Idem.*
[119] *Idem.*
[120] *Idem.*

[121]*Idem.*
[122]*Idem.*
[123]*Idem*
[124]*Idem.*
[125]*Idem.*
[126]*Idem.*
[127]*Idem.*
[128]MMR-2-Book 1 – Decree no. 2, recorded in the book of transgressions in 17.09.1801.
[129]MMR-2-Book 1 – 28.03.1808.
[130]*Idem.*
[131]*Idem.*
[132]ANTT – Arquive of the Kindom's Office, packet 281; MMR-38.
[133]MMR-2-Book 1 – 17.10.1808 – Letter sent by the Surveyor-General to Rio de Janeiro.
[134]*Idem.*
[135]MMR-2-Book 1 – 1809 to 1812.
[136]MMR, nos. 2, 37 and 38 (1777-1721).
[137]Silbert, op. cit., petition no. 15a, p. 118.
[138]Idem, petition no. 88b, p. 101.
[139]Correia, José Eduardo Horta – *Liberalismo e Catolicismo: O Problema Congreganista (1820-1823)*, Coimbra, Universidade de Coimbra, 1974.
[140]*Diário das Cortes Gerais e Extraordinárias da Nação Portuguesa*, Imprensa Nacional, 1821-1823; Session from 18.08.1821.
[141]*Idem.*
[142]The park of Vila Viçosa belonged to the House of Bragança, not to the Crown.
[143]*Diário das Cortes*, op. cit., session from 18.08.1821.
[144]*Idem.*
[145]*Idem.*
[146]*Diário das Cortes*, op. cit., session from August 18th 1821.
[147]Licence from July 24th 1824.
[148]Gaspar, Jorge – *A Área de Influência de Évora. Sistemas de Funções e Lugares Centrais*, Lisbon, CEG/INIC, 1972.
[149]MMR-2-Book 1 – 10.05.1791.
[150]MMR-2-Book 1 – 25.06.1787; 30.12.1791.
[151]MMR-2-Book 1 – 28.09.1802.
[152]MMR-17 – 1777 – Licences granted to two inhabitants at the same time in 18.08.1777.
[153]MMR-2-Book 1 – 27.05.1777; *Gazeta de Lisboa* – 18.06.1787-; D. Fernando José de Melo "Noble Men of Her Majesty's House" and heir to the House of Surveyor-Generals, inaugurates the post of Surveyor-General on May 27th 1777, post which he will occupy for ten years until death, on January 29th 1787.
[154]Câncio, Francisco – *Ribatejo Histórico e Monumental*, Santarém, 1938, p. 145; *Gazeta de Lisboa* – from 1777 to 1794.
[155]Beirão, Caetano – *D. Maria I* – quoted by Francisco Câncio in op. cit., p. 145.
[156]MMR-16-1778 – In 07.08.1778, the woodkeeper of the Pinheiro reserve informs the Surveyor-General about a fire set in that reserve; in 09.12.1778, the judge at the Muja reserve sends the Surveyor-General a similar information about 3 fires set at the same time in Muja.
[157]These averages were calculated by the analysis of sundry letters exchanged between officers and the Surveyor-General, and exclusively regard nucleus 16. The Correspondence Copy Book of nucleus 2, MMR-2-Book, has less information than that of nucleus 16.
[158]MMR-16-1778 and 1784 – Grant of licences to the inhabitants of the reserves of Pera e Comporta in 02.06.1778; grant of licence to the Abbot of the Monastery of S. Bento de Santarém to cut down wood destined to "repair two barns, repair the stables and houses, and use in the kitchen"; grant of licences to the inhabitants of Óbidos in 24.10.1784.
[159]*Gazeta de Lisboa* – 18.06.1787; *Gazeta de Lisboa* – 31.01.1789.
[160]D. Francisco José da Cunha Mendonça e Meneses, heir to the Lords of Valdigem, future 1st Count of Castro Marim in 1802, Governor of Arms of Alentejo and the Algarve, 1st Marquis of Olhão in 1808, is one of the names glorified for having been the head of the rebellion against the French in 1808; *Gazeta de Lisboa* – 31.01.1789; Pinto, Albano da Silveira – *Resenha das Famílias e Titulares e Grandes de Portugal*, Lisboa, vol. II, pp. 183-184; Acúrsio, op. cit.; Valente, Vasco Pulido – "O Povo em Armas: a Revolta Nacional de 1808-1809" in *Análise Social*, 2nd Series, vol. XV (57), 1979, 1st, pp. 7-48.

[161] From 1794 onwards, from D. Maria I's illness and the establishment of the royal family in Queluz, hunting journeys become less frequent. During D. Maria I's whole reign, the *Gazeta de Lisboa* reported every year Her Majesty's winter journeys to game reserves and how often she went to the royal residence of Salvaterra.

[162] MMR-17-1791 to 1792 – 25.02.1791: Ten "cart-loads of cork-trees for the army's warehouses"; 25.06.92: Queen's order for the woodkeeper of the Pinheiro reserve to mark the pinetrees and "royal branches at the reserve of Alcácer and the ones that should be kept for the Navy".

[163] MMR-2-Book 1 – 20.05.1790 – Licence granted to D. Diana to farm the "mentioned ground" at the reserve of Almeirim; 26.06.1790 – Licence granted to reduce the vineyard and olive grove "in a ground near the properties of the Real Colegiada de Santarém".

[164] MMR-2- Book 1 – Opinion of the Surveyor-General about a ground at the Charneca de Vale de Tijolos, reserve of Almeirim, given to Gerardo Vencislau Braancamp de Almeida Castelo Branco (member of the agriculture council).

[165] MMR-2-Book 1 – 31.03.1975.

[166] MMR-2-Book 1 – 29.11.1799.

[167] MMR-2-Book 1 – 19.11.1799.

[168] Vandelli, Domingos – "Plano de uma Lei agrária" in *Aritmética Política e Finanças 1770-1804*, Lisbon, Banco de Portugal, 1994.

[169] "Speech to be read at the session of the shipping society, honoured with the presence of His Royal Highness the Prince Regent our Lord", in Coutinho, Rodrigo de Souza – *Textos Políticos, Económicos e Financeiros 1783-1811*, Tomo II, Lisbon, Banco de Portugal, 1993.

[170] MMR-2-Book 1 – 17.03.1801.

[171] *Idem.*

[172] *Idem.*

[173] *Idem.*

[174] *Idem.*

[175] *Idem.*

[176] *Idem.*

[177] *Idem.*

[178] *Idem.*

[179] MMR-2-Book 1 – 28.09.1802.

[180] *Idem.*

[181] *Idem.*

[182] MMR-2-Book 1 – 04.11.1802.

[183] *Idem.*

[184] Coutinho, Rodrigo de Souza, op. cit.

[185] *Idem.*

[186] MMR-2-Book 1 – 17.03.1801.

[187] MMR-2-Book 1 – 20.04.1805.

[188] MMR-2-Book 1 – 03.02.1806.

[189] MMR-2-Book 1 – 23.10.1806.

[190] MMR-2-Book 1 – 23.10.1806.

[191] MMR-2-Book 1 – 13.07.1807.

[192] Neves, José Acúrsio, op. cit.

[193] Neves, José Acúrsio, op. cit.

[194] MMR-2-Book 1 – 26.04.1808.

[195] MMR-2-Book 1 – 26.04.1808.

[196] MMR-31-1808 – Report from Beja – Purveyor's office – 30.04.1808; Report from Elvas – Purveyor's office – 01.05.1808; Report from Setúbal – Purveyor's office – 04.05.1808; Report from Castelo Branco – Purveyor's office – 04.05.1808; Report from Lamego – Purveyor's office – 04.05.1808; Report from Santarém – Purveyor's office – 04.05.1808; Report from the Algarve – Purveyor's office – 04.05.1808; Report from Tomar – Purveyor's office – 05.05.1808; Report from Aveiro – Purveyor's office – 04.05.1808; Report from Torres Vedras – Purveyor's office – no date.

[197] MMR-2-Book 1 – 24.09.1808.

[198] MMR-2-Book 1 – 26.06.1809 – "the most scandalous and absolute freedom of hunting at their own wish, doing without reserve laws that they say no longer exist, publicly invading all places, killing all kinds of game and using wood, thickets and firewood (…) indispensable to royal service for the supply of the Navy's and Army's Royal Warehouses."

[199] MMR-2-Book 1 – 27.10.1810.

[200] MMR-2-Book 1 – 10.12.1809.
[201] MMR-2-Book 1 – 17.10.1808.
[202] ANTT – Archive of the Kingdom's Office, packet 281.
[203] Silbert, op. cit. – petition no. 13b, pp. 112-113.
[204] MMR-2-Book 2 – 05.04.1816 – Licences to fell woods for the inhabitants of Valada.
[205] MMR-2-Book 2 – 07.01.1816; 15.02.1817 – Order to hunt wolves granted to the judge, town councillors and council officials of the reserve of Vimieiro, 15.07.1817.
[206] MMR-2-Book 2 – 21.03.1816 – Letter sent by the Surveyor-General to the judge of Salvaterra and Benavente for guards to prevent cattle from entering reserves.
[207] MMR-2-Book 2 – 03.06.1817 – Information and payment order on the firebreaks ordered by the patrol corporal of Salvaterra de Magos.
[208] MMR-2-Book 2 – 1812-1833; MMR-16 – 1820-1821.
[209] Bulletin from the Direcção-Geral de Agricultura (Directorate General for Agriculture), 8th year, no. 8, part I, Lisbon, Imprensa Nacional, 1908.
[210] MMR-16 – 1778 – 02.06.1778 – Letter from the Surveyor-General to the Judge of Setúbal informing him of the grace granted to the inhabitants of Pera e Comporta.
[211] MMR-2-Book 1 – Letters sent to the reserve judge of Salvaterra and Benavente in 13.05.1791 and 04.06.1796.
[212] *Ibidem.*
[213] *Idem.*
[214] MMR-30 – 1777 to 1821.
[215] *Idem.*
[216] MMR-2-Book 1 (1777-1812) and Book 2 (1812-1821).
[217] MMR-2-Book 1 – Letter sent by the Surveyor-General, D. Fernando José de Melo, to the Duke of Cadaval in 02.12.1782.
[218] MMR-14 – Record of hunting licences between 1777 and 1821.
[219] *Gazeta de Lisboa*, 1777-1800.
[220] MMR-2-Book 1 – Hunting licence granted to the woodkeeper of Pera e Comporta to hunt mallards at the fen, in 27.02.1782; and to the royal administrator of Comporta in 05.03.1787; Licences granted in 27.02.82, 25.11.82, and 20.08.83.
[221] MMR-2-Book 1 – Letter sent to the reserve judge of the reserves of Santarém.
[222] MMR-2-Books 1 and 2, 1810-1815.
[223] Pérez Vicente, Isabel – "Legislación cinegética en España: Evolución y Actualidad" in *Agricultura y Sociedad*, no. 58, Enero-Marzo, 1991, pp. 173-213.
[224] Nahon, Guillaume – *La Révolution et la Chasse*, Union Nationale des Fédérations Départementales.
[225] Argote de Molina, Gonzalo – *Discurso sobre la Monteria, 1582 (Con outro Discurso y notas del Exmo. Señor D. José Gutierrez de la Vega* – Single Volume, Madrid, 1882; "Aviso de Caçadores e Caça. Ordenado por el Doctor Nuñez de Avenduño; Letrado de Don Yñigo Lopez de Mendonça Tercero deste Nombre, Duque del Infantado", 1593; Faria, Manuel Severim de – *Discursos Vários Políticos, por Manuel Severim de Faria, novamente reimpressos e corrigidos segundo a edição de 1624*, Lisbon, Imprensa Régia, 1805; Martínez de Espinar, Alonso – *Arte de Ballesteria y Montería*, Madrid, 1644.
[226] Nuñez de Avenduño, op. cit.
[227] Gama, L. A. Ludovice da – *Resumo da Caça Ordinária, Poesia e Siência do Caçador Rústico*, Lisbon, Typografia da Gazeta de Portugal, 1866.
[228] *Idem.*
[229] Lopez Ontiveros, Antonio – "Algunos Aspectos de la Evolución de la Caza en España" – in *Agricultura y Sociedad*, no. 58, Enero-Marzo, 1991, pp. 47-51.
[230] Faria, Manuel Severim de, op. cit.
[231] Lopez Ontiveros, op. cit.; Pérez Vicente, Isabel, op. cit.
[232] Perrin, Beneton de – *Eloge Historique de la Chasse*, Paris, Morel le jeune, grand'salle du Palais an grand Cyrus; Gonuchon, rue de la Huchette, Briasson, rue de S. Jacques, à la Science, Guillaume, quai des Augustins à saint Charles, 1824 (1st edition 1734).
[233] Nahon, Guillaume, op. cit.
[234] Carvalho, Porfírio, op. cit.
[235] Oliveira, Luiz da Silva Pereira – *Privilégios da Nobreza e Fidalguia de Portugal*, Lisbon, 1806. This author considers two ranks of nobility: natural and civil.
[236] See the Lisbon's museum catalogue.
[237] *Museo del Prado*, 1990.
[238] *Idem.*

[239] Chevalier, Jean; Gheerbrant, Alain – *Dicionário dos Símbolos*, Lisbon, Círculo de Leitores, 1997.
[240] Pijoan, J. – *Arte Universal*, vol. 6, Lisbon, Alfa, 1989, p. 225.
[241] Information conveyed by João Bugalho, hunter and professional sylviculturist.
[242] *Livro da Montaria Feito por D. João I de Portugal* – Preface by Francisco Maria Pereira, Coimbra, Imprensa da Universidade, 1918.
[243] Grassby, Ricard, op. cit.; Guedes, Natália Correia, op. cit.
[244] Grassby, Ricard, op. cit.
[245] Guedes, Natália Correia, op. cit.; (MMR-2, MMR-10 and MMR-11-1783-1796).
[246] Guedes, Natália Correia, op. cit.
[247] MMR-3-1777-1800; MMR-11-1777-1806; MMR-2-1800-1810.
[248] MMR-2-Book 1-1783-1796.
[249] MMR-2-Book 1-1777-1799.
[250] BNL-RES – "Descrição das Coutadas e Casas de Campo dos Príncipes de Portugal" in cod. 10768, no date, no year, fol. 215 v.º-217.
[251] *Idem.*
[252] *Idem.*
[253] *Idem.*
[254] *Gazeta de Lisboa*, 1794.
[255] *Gazeta de Lisboa*, 1795-1796.
[256] MMR-28-1778-1786; *Gazeta de Lisboa*, 1778-1793.
[257] *Gazeta de Lisboa*, 1778-1800; MMR-28-1778-1786.
[258] MMR-28-1777-1789.
[259] *Idem.*
[260] MMR-16-1781-15.08.1781 – Letter sent to the Surveyor-General by the reserve judge of Sintra.
[261] MMR-16-1780-21.11.1780; MMR-2-Book 1-15.11.1781; 06.12.1783 and 20.12.1781 (cleaning ways through the woods at Salvaterra de Magos and Samora); 27.10.1785; 13.10.1787; 10.12.1789; 29.05.89 (to repair the bridges at the reserves of Óbidos).
[262] MMR-2-Book 1-18.12.1781; 11.12.1783; 10.11.1785; 22.12.1788; 26.11.89; 03.12.1790; 19.11.1791; MMR-17-1788-1789-23.04.1788 (Felling for the royal pantry of Caldas); 16.07.1789 (stay at Sintra); 22.12.1788 (for the 1789 stay at Salvaterra).
[263] ANTT – Archive of the Royal House – L.512.
[264] *Gazeta de Lisboa*, 1790-1800.
[265] MMR-38-1777-1815.
[266] MMR-16-1777-1792.
[267] MMR-2-Book 1-04.06.1779.
[268] MMR-38-1779 – Inquiry on Aldeia Galega and Alcochete.
[269] MMR-38 – Inquiry on the reserve of Coruche, held in 27.03.1779.
[270] MMR-38 – Inquiry on the reserves of the Setúbal circuit, held in 01.06.1779.
[271] Idem – testimony of António Rodrigues, worker, in 31.07.1779.
[272] MMR-38 – Investigation process of Setúbal, in 01.06.1779.
[273] MMR-16-1779-22.06.1779 – Report sent to the Surveyor-General by the gamekeeper of Santarém.
[274] MMR-16-1780-11.06.1780 – Report on the inquiry of Benavente sent to the Surveyor-General by the Judge of Santarém.
[275] MMR-16-1780-18.06.1780 – Testimonies from the judges of Salvaterra and the gamekeeper of Santarém.
[276] MMR-16-1778-25.02.1778.
[277] MMR-2-Book 1-19.06.1777.
[278] Data from MMR-2-Book 1-19.06.1779 and 28.02.1781.
[279] MMR-2-Book 1 – 16.04.1782.
[280] MMR-2-Book 1 – 23.05.1782.
[281] MMR-2-Book 1 – 01.04.1782 and 04.07.1781; 04.05.1783 – Order to the judge of Sintra to slaughter the dogs found inside reserves and not useful for royal packs.
[282] MMR-2-Book 1 – 05.12.1781.
[283] MMR-2-Book 1 – Order sent to the reserve judge of Samora and Belmonte, Joaquim Ferreira, to arrest the gamekeeper Miguel António Vieira.
[284] MMR-2-Book 1 – 18.05.1787.
[285] MMR-2-Book 1 – 24.07.1789.
[286] MMR-2-Book 1 – 31.03.1795.
[287] MMR-2-Book 1 – 08.08.1796.

[288]MMR-2-Book 1 – 20.10.1799.

[289]Sources available on this process have gaps between 1805 and 1811, year of the publication the Historical Memory made by the lord of Pancas, where his side of the facts is presented. Daun, Joseph S. de Saldanha Oliveira – *Memoria Historica sobre A Origem, Progresso, e Consequencias da Famoza Cauza da Denuncia de Pancas; que no Juizo da regia Corôa de Portuga, Ofereceu a Viuva D. Maria Balbina de Souza Coutinho contra os Actuais Senhores de pancasD. Maria Leonor Manuel de Vilhena Costa Freire, e Seu Marido*, London, H. Byer, Blackfriars, 1811.

[290]MMR-37-1805 – 26.08.1805 – Summary of the inquiry process of the reserve of Belas.

[291]MMR-2-Book 1 – 15.02.1809 – Letter sent by the Surveyor-General to the judge of Salvaterra.

[292]MMR-2-Book 1 – 03.02.1809.

[293]MMR-2-Book 2 – 24.12.1812.

[294]MMR-2-Book 2 – 12.05.1812.

[295]MMR-2-Book 2 – 09.10.1813 – Letter sent by D. Pedro da Cunha to general Peacok, "Commander of the British troops in Lisbon".

[296]MMR-2-Book 2 – 09.10.1813.

[297]MMR-2-Book 2 – 14.10.1813.

[298]MMR-16-1821.

[299]Regulations of 1605, § 41.

[300]MMR-38-1777 and 1795 – Investigation report in Salvaterra on the fires raised in royal reserves; 1795 – Salvaterra de Magos – instrument of civil appeal to find out whether it was possible or not to grow products at the reserve.

[301]MMR-2-Book 2 – 09.11.1814.

[302]MMR-2-Book 2 – 21.03.1816; MMR-2-Book 2 – 31.03.1818.

[303]MMR-2-Book 1 – 27.11.1781.

[304]MMR-2-Book 1 – 1777-1821.

[305]MMR-2-Book 1-1777 – 30.11.1777.

[306]MMR-38 – Inquiries set at the royal reserves between 1777 and 1789.

[307]MMR-2-Book 1 – 23.10.1799.

[308]MMR-2-Book 1 – 19.11.1799.

[309]MMR-16-1781 – 02.09.1781 – Letter sent by the reserve judge of Óbidos to the Surveyor-General.

[310]MMR-2-Book 1 – 24.07.1786.

[311]MMR-17-1795 – 18.05.1795 – Letter sent by the reserve judge of Óbidos to the Surveyor-General.

[312]MMR-2-Book 1 – 23.01.1798.

[313]MMR-2-Book 1 – 15.10.1813.

[314]See Chapter 2.

[315]MMR-2-Book 1 – 27.01.1812.

[316]MMR-2-Book 1 – 08.02.1812.

[317]MMR-2-Book 2 – 06.06.1814.

[318]MMR-2-Book 2 – 14.01.1815.

[319]MMR-16-1819 – 29.11.1819.

[320]MMR-16-1821 – 28.02.1821.

[321]MMR-16-1821 – 17.07.1821.

[322]On nobility, aristocratic *ethos*, Court behaviour patterns and rules in Portugal by the end of the Ancient Regime see Monteiro, Nuno Gonçalo Pimenta de Freitas – *O Crepúsculo dos Grandes (1750-1832)*, Lisbon, Imprensa Nacional Casa da Moeda, 1998.

[323]*Idem*.

[324]On agrarian movements, see Tengarrinha, op. cit.

[325]Freeman, Michael, op. cit. and Thompson, E. P., op. cit.

[326]MMR-2-Book 1 – 27.05.1777.

[327]ANTT – Registo Geral das Mercês (General Register of Mercês).

[328]*Gazeta de Lisboa* – 31.01.1789 and ANTT – Registo Geral das Mercês.

[329]*Gazeta de Lisboa* – 20.02.1789.

[330]Fernandes, Paulo Jorge – *As Faces de Proteu: Elites Urbanas e Poder Municipal em Lisboa de Finais do Século XVIII a 1851*, Lisbon, Câmara Municipal de Lisboa, 1999.

www.ingramcontent.com/pod-product-compliance
Lightning Source LLC
Chambersburg PA
CBHW080856230426
43662CB00013B/2120